P9-DTE-375

FROM THE LAND OF SHEBA

FROM THE LAND OF SHEBA

TALES OF THE JEWS OF YEMEN

NEW AND REVISED EDITION

COLLECTED AND EDITED BY

S. D. GOITEIN

SCHOCKEN BOOKS · NEW YORK

Copyright © 1947, 1973 by Schocken Books Inc.
Library of Congress Catalog Card No. 73-81342
Manufactured in the United States of America

TALES TRANSLATED BY CHRISTOPHER FREMANTLE

COLLECTED AND EDITED BY

TABLE OF CONTENTS

Preface

"Operation Magic Carpet," the airlift in 1949–50 of practically all the Jews who had remained in Yemen to the newly founded State of Israel, was regarded by the participants as a miracle. It was indeed a fantastic achievement, considering that the emigrants had to be assembled from about eleven hundred localities which were not connected by any means of modern communications. In Israel, the Yemenites form a small fraction of the population, probably not more than 4 per cent. But their distinctive features, their industry, spirituality, and other amiable traits, their handicrafts and dances have attracted the attention of their fellow citizens, of visitors, and of scholars. Much has been written about them, a good deal by Yemenites themselves.

Whoever had the opportunity, like the present writer, to observe immigrants from the villages of Yemen during the early 1930's, or to visit the reception camp near Aden, South Arabia, in 1949, and to meet the same people years later in Israel, would be impressed by their transformation. The individual differences are great. But despite enormous economic, social, and spiritual handicaps, as a whole, the Yemenites have adapted well to Israel. The recent election of a Yemenite, born and bred in Yemen, to the prestigious position of speaker of the Knesset, Israel's parliament, might serve as an indication.

This volume is not concerned with the acculturation of the Yemenites, but with the opposite: their life and mentality while still in their native country. The powerful autobiographic account "A Good-for-Nothing," taken down by me from the mouth of a young man shortly after his arrival in Palestine, in 1929, immediately plunges the reader into a thoroughly tradition-bound society—strange, almost bizarre, but eminently human. The two following pieces are taken from the book of a Jewish coopersmith describing life in the countryside about one hundred years ago, when it was dominated by the stern customary law of the tribes. From a slightly earlier period comes the loving picture of the immensely learned blacksmith and his three wives.

The story and the jest reproduced in the second part of the book belong to the repertoire of women's entertainment and are part and parcel of the common literary heritage of the Middle East. But the often humoristic Aggadot, or Hebrew wise sayings, and the stories of physicians and other learned men have specific Yemenite flavor.

The songs of the women, especially of the villagers, possess great charm, but, not unlike classical Arabic poetry, often contain allusions to local personalities and events, and consequently require commentaries, which would be out of place in a book of this type. I hope the song of the little shepherdess on page 92 will show the reader what he has missed.

The third and concluding part is not intended to illustrate the history of the Yemenites as it really was but as it was reflected in their minds before they became acquainted with the results of modern research. The stories reproduced are either Midrashim, that is, imaginative elaborations of biblical passages or legends with a moralistic tendency or, with regard to more recent times, factual, albeit often incorrect, traditions.

In the introductory essay I try to reconstruct the history of the Jews in Yemen on the basis of reliable sources and to outline their spiritual heritage. Advice for further reading is provided at the end of the book.

S. D. GOITEIN

FROM THE LAND OF SHEBA

About the Jews of Yemen

When I visited the ancient seaport of Aden in 1949 in order to observe the mass exodus of the Jews from Yemen, I had opportunity to admire the beautiful native sailing boats, and it occurred to me that the vessels sent there by King Solomon three thousand years ago might have looked much the same. The biblical accounts prove that the kings of Judea were eager to follow the example of King Solomon in order to safeguard a continuous supply of South-Arabian incense, then used in every temple and every better household (just as another Arabian substance, of a less good smell, however, is presently in demand all over the world). Thus it is highly likely that Jews visited Yemen from the early times of Israel's kingdom, and some might have settled there in a traders' colony. But no written record with regard to Jews permanently settled in Yemen has come down to us from those remote times.

The first trustworthy and substantial testimony to the Jewish presence in South Arabia is provided by inscriptions. The most surprising discovery was made only a few years ago (in 1969): a bi-lingual inscription, written partly in the local language and partly in Hebrew. It was found in an environment where Jews had lived from time immemorial until they left the country. The inscription tells about a building erected by a man whose first name was Judah "with the help and charity of his Lord, the creator of his soul, the Lord of the living and the dead, the Lord of heaven and earth, who created everything; and with the support of his people Israel [that is, the Jews]; and by the authority of the king of Sheba [name and titles supplied]; and by the authority of his tribal lord." The building served both as a domicile and a sanctuary. Because the Jews are mentioned before the king and the tribal lord, it stands to reason that Jews had contributed to the construction of the building, which probably served also as the local synagogue. In Yemen, synagogues were mostly private foundations, simply a large room inside a family mansion, often equipped through donations of persons other than the founder. The name of the king, known from other sources, and the script of the inscription indicate that it was engraved in the fourth Christian century, that is, over two hundred years before Mohammed founded the new religion of Islam in the northern part of Arabia. Our inscription already betrays a trend of Jewish religious propaganda which later became the cornerstone of Mohammed's Islam: the concern with the soul and life after death and the concept of God the creator, who is able to resurrect the dead and to punish those who deserve it.

Other monotheistic inscriptions from South Arabia call God "The All-merciful," the name common in the Talmud and later adopted by Islam, and some describe him expressly as "God of the Jews." Muslim sources contain legends about South-Arabian kings embracing Judaism, especially about the last one, Joseph As'ar, "the one with the side-curls." On the basis of these accounts it has become customary to speak about a Jewish kingdom in pre-Islamic Yemen, which has led to the assumption that the Yemenite Jews descend from natives converted to Judaism, about which more will be said later. Concerning the alleged Judaism of the kings of Yemen, new insights were gained in the 1950's after the discovery of inscriptions from Joseph As'ar's entourage. These inscriptions indeed represent a monotheistic religion; they even preach, as Islam later did, a Holy War until the entire world would acknowledge the rule of the All-merciful. But this religion was tied to a local temple, called after a pagan deity, just as Mohammed sincerely believed that he proclaimed the religion of the People of the Book but remained attached to the sanctuary of his native city of Mecca. Yemen had not become a Jewish kingdom; rather it was temporarily (and only partly) ruled by a Judaizing Arab religion, which, unlike Islam, did not last, because the country was conquered by the Christian Abyssinians, who were backed by the mighty Byzantine war machine. But I have little doubt that had Joseph, "the one with the side-curls," succeeded, the Jews would not have fared better under him than they did under Mohammed and his successors.

By the time of the advent of Islam the Jewish population of Yemen must have been already considerable and most probably dispersed all over the country, as we find it throughout the centuries until the very end. This alone seems to explain the strange fact that the Muslims expelled the Christians but not the Jews from Yemen. Islamic law does not discriminate between Jews and Christians. But the Christians in Yemen were merchants living in Sanaa, the capital, and in Najran, the seat of a bishop. It was easy to get hold of them and to send them out of the country; Muslim traders would be only too eager to take their place. But craftsmen dispersed in many different localities were less conspicuous, difficult to assemble, and even more difficult to replace. Anyhow we know that this socio-economic factor accounted for the survival of the Jews under Islam in Yemen for 1,360 years, though they lived in the humiliating and precarious state of a "protected" minority within a chaotic and fervently religious society.

The very first document written on paper referring to the Jews of Yemen shows them dispersed all over the country to a far higher degree even than they were at the time of their mass exodus in 1949–50. Jewish settlements reached deep into the country known today as the kingdom of Saudi Arabia and all through central Arabia. In this way, a continuous link was created between the Jews of Yemen and those of Iraq, ancient Babylonia, which, at that time, the ninth and tenth centuries, was the spiritual center of Judaism.

Here a word on the origin of the Jews of Yemen must be said. Like all Jews, their original stock had come from Palestine. An unbroken chain of Jewish settlements stretching from Palestine southward through Arabia is known from both inscriptions and literary sources. Moreover, the Yemenites' ways of life, as they were observed and described in detail first by Jacob Safir in his travelogue (see page 58), bear astounding similarity to those of the Talmudic sages from Palestine. The advent of Islam severed the connections between Palestine and Yemen, for non-Muslims were (and are) not permitted to travel through northwestern Arabia, the cradle of the new

4

religion. Yemenite Jewry had to look to Iraq for spiritual guidance. But internecine wars, bad administration, and other misfortunes impoverished Iraq, and many of its people, Muslims and Jews alike, emigrated. As Professor Shlomo Morag, of the Hebrew University, and other scholars have proved, the pronunciation of Hebrew of the Yemenite Jews is that of Babylonia, and they, more than any other Jewish tribe, have preserved the traditions of the Babylonian schools. Thus there can be little doubt that the originally Palestinian core of Jews in Yemen was replenished by a generous supply of immigrants from Iraq. It must be noted also that the royal house of the Imams, or heads of the Zaidi sect, who ruled Yemen for a thousand years, also emigrated from Iraq to Yemen in the tenth century. It is likely that Jews were found in their service, for the Zaidi lawbooks, written in Iraq, contain much material about the treatment of *dhimmis,* or "protected people."

To come back to a question raised earlier. It is entirely possible that some persons in pre-Islamic South Arabia embraced the Jewish religion (not the Arabian Judaizing monotheism described before). If so, these persons must have been entirely absorbed within the genuine Jewish community, for the population of Yemen became Muslim in Mohammed's lifetime, and during the 1,360 years that have elapsed between that event and the exodus of the Jews from Yemen, apostasy from Islam was punished with the death penalty, that is, was practically impossible. How a native population converted to Judaism fares is demonstrated by the Falashas, who live in the

5

mountains on the other side of the Red Sea; they know next to nothing about Judaism, while the Yemenites are the most Jewish of Jews.

In addition to the two successive groups of Jewish immigrants to Yemen, from Palestine and from Iraq, both traveling mainly by land, a third came later by sea: Jews from Persia (Iran), attracted by the India trade, which by the eleventh century preferred the southern route via Aden, South Arabia, instead of, as before, Iraq, which had become too turbulent.

The India trade was the backbone of medieval international economy. As everyone knows, America was discovered because Columbus was looking for a direct seaway to India. In medieval conditions the products of India and the Far East were not mere luxuries. Take the staple good: pepper. There were no refrigerators in those days, and in order to preserve meat and other food pepper was needed. Likewise, little was known about chemically produced medicaments, but the knowledge of medicinal plants was very extensive, and most of such plants came from India and the Far East. Finally, those medieval people, men not less than women, loved colorful garments; they looked indeed like tropical songbirds. And again, ignorant of synthetic dyes, they had to have recourse to natural coloring stuffs which mostly came from those remote regions.

This great India trade, which reached its zenith—as far as Jewish participation is concerned—in the twelfth century, united Jews from all the Muslim countries, which served as intermediaries between the Orient and

Europe: besides Iran and Iraq, Egypt, Palestine, and Syria, as well as the countries of the western Mediterranean, Spain, Morocco, Tunisia, and Libya, and the islands of Majorca and Sicily. The merchants assembled in Aden, where the main exchange of goods took place, but many proceeded farther to one of the twenty or so ports of India which we know Jews visited. Some particularly daring travelers went as far as Indonesia, to the island of Sumatra, where the priceless but much needed camphor was found. They did not go to China, for in that period the Chinese did not admit foreign merchants.

These were the great days of the Jews of Yemen. A Muslim source tells us that the customs tariff of Aden, "which will stand until the Day of Resurrection," was fixed by a Jew from Persia. According to the same source, another Jew dug one of those wells which provided the water supply of the growing port city. The representative of the merchants and superintendent of the port in the second quarter of the twelfth century was a scholarly scion of a Persian Jewish family whose father had preceded him in his capacity as head of the merchants. The son was called Madmun, a name still common among Yemenites (it is the Arabic equivalent of Shemaryahu, both meaning God-protected). Madmun was a partner of a Muslim merchant who later became the ruler of southern Yemen. Together with his partner Madmun built a large ship and fitted it out for the long voyage of two thousand miles on the direct route from Aden to Ceylon. On its maiden voyage, the ship carried among

7

its passengers three Jewish goldsmiths, at least one (but probably all) of them from North Africa, a detail not without interest for the history of the small arts.

In the same letter in which Madmun reports about this great maritime venture, he notes that he had sent simultaneously sixty bales of dyeing stuff, together with pepper, Ceylonese cinnamon, and Oriental textiles, westward from Aden to Egypt. He also sent a substantial gift to a bereaved family in Tripoli, Libya, whose father had drowned in the sea of Aden.

Madmun's letter just mentioned and hundreds of others referring to the India trade have been found in the so-called Cairo Geniza, about which something must be said here since it is almost our only source for the history of the Jews of Yemen until the end of the High Middle Ages. A *geniza* is a place where discarded sacred writings are put aside in order to preserve them from desecration. This was general Jewish custom and still is observed in Orthodox Jewish communities throughout the world. The Cairo Geniza, that is, a lumber room in a synagogue in Old Cairo serving that purpose, was exceptional in that secular papers, such as letters, legal documents, and accounts, were deposited there alongside religious and other literary writings. Over the centuries this material became completely mixed up, and the confusion was enhanced by its dispersion among many libraries in Europe, the United States, and Israel. The result is that the beginning of a letter found in Leningrad might have its continuation in Cambridge, England, and the end in New York. During twenty years of Geniza research I succeeded in assembling over three hundred and fifty letters and documents related to the India trade, many of them connected in one way or another with Aden and Yemen. The Geniza has also preserved some writings of Yemenites who had settled in Egypt, in Jerusalem, and even in faraway Morocco.

The Geniza letters of the Yemenite Jews, those writing from Aden as well as those from inland Yemen, betray a fine standard of culture. Their Arabic is pleasant, their Hebrew learned; their general style is urbane, even refined. Yemen is an alpine country, where travel is difficult and the distances are great. From Sa'da, then the largest northermost Jewish settlement in Yemen, to Aden was a twelve days' donkey ride. Yet we find a visitor from Sa'da honored in Aden by being allowed to lead the community in prayer on a holiday. The visitor also reports that his hometown followed the instructions of Madmun, the representative of the merchants of Aden, with regard to the rites of the public service. From other letters, too, we learn that despite the difficulty of communications, Yemen's dispersed Jewish settlements closely cooperated with one another.

At that time, the first half of the twelfth century, the royal court had moved from the capital, Sanaa, which is situated in the highland in the center of the country, to Dhu Gibla in the southern hill country, according to Muslim sources originally a Jewish potters' village. The Jews of Sanaa and those of two other old congregations settled in the new seat of government. A letter, written in the name of these three Jewish congregations of Dhu Gibla to Aden has been preserved in the Geniza. But how astounded was I when I heard the names of two of them from the mouths of immigrants in the early 1950's and their original places described as *roesh golus,* or "spearheads of the exiled," that is, Jewish settlements founded in Yemen immediately after their exodus from the Holy Land. I pondered: if an oral tradition can last from the twelfth to the twentieth century, there is no reason why it should not have persisted from the third or fourth to the twelfth.

The coherence of the Jewish congregations in Yemen was rooted in local as well as in ecumenical needs. The Jews settled their legal affairs, such as marriage, divorce, inheritance, and also commercial disputes, between themselves, but only in large centers, such as the inland capital or Aden, was there a sufficient number of scholars able to act as a high court to decide more difficult cases. In order to ensure efficiency and their own position, Jewish local leaders tried to be recognized by the ecumenical Jewish authorities. Here they got into trouble. Because of the close connection of Yemen with Iraq and the emigration of Persian Jews to Aden, the Jewish ecumenical authority recognized by the Yemenites was in Baghdad. He was the Head of the Diaspora, who claimed to be a descendant of King David, and the *gaons,* or presidents of the two Babylonian yeshivas, or high councils.

But the India trade, on which Aden and Yemen lived, had turned to the West. The closest connections, business and family ties, existed between the leading Yemenite merchants and those of the Mediterranean basin. Madmun, the representative of the merchants in

10

Aden, was married to the sister of Judah ben Joseph ha-Kohen, the Jewish representative of the merchants in Old Cairo; the latter's wife was a sister of a shipowner from Aden; another Adenese, a cousin of Madmun, of whose correspondence much has been preserved, also was a relative of Judah. The traffic of goods and spouses between the Mediterranean and Aden was paralleled by that of books, Jewish scholarship, and Hebrew poetry. Once again, Yemenite Jewry began to look westward for spiritual leadership. In 1127 the *gaon*, or head of the Jerusalem yeshiva, moved to Cairo and was recognized by the Fatimid calif as the highest Jewish authority in his empire. The ruler of Yemen—a queen—had acknowledged the suzeranity of the Fatimid calif of Cairo by the late eleventh century. Considering all these circumstances, Madmun ordered the Jewish communities in Yemen to mention in public prayer the name of the head of the yeshiva of the Holy Land, who now had his seat in Cairo, after that of the Head of the Diaspora, who had his seat in Baghdad.

Then, something extraordinary occured. In spring, 1134, a Persian Jew, a relative of the Head of the Diaspora, appeared in Aden, claimed and received recognition as highest Jewish authority in the country and abolished the prayer for the Palestinian *gaon*. This is a telling example of Jewish autonomy within medieval Islam. Although southern Yemen recognized the Fatimid calif of Cairo, the Jews there were not afraid of swearing allegiance to a Jewish authority in a country under the rule of a rival calif. This attitude was not an expression of defiance on the side of the

Jews or of tolerance on the side of the rulers; rather, the government did not care what its subjects did, as long as they paid their taxes and caused no trouble.

In the light of this explanation the events in Aden in spring, 1134, have to be understood. When, after Passover, the merchants from the Mediterranean area, who were dedicated to the Palestinian gaonate, arrived in Aden, some setting out from Egypt and some returning from India, where they had passed the winter, and heard what had happened, they became furious and even threatened to apply to the government. Such an appeal would have been fraught with perils, and it was not carried out. Instead, a complicated internal struggle ensued, about which the Geniza has much to report. The strife was assuaged by rich presents sent by the merchants of Aden to the head and other members of the Palestinian yeshiva. Concurrently with the donations from Aden, the yearly dues vowed to the yeshiva by the congregations of inland Yemen were properly collected, delivered, and forwarded.

Here a word about the material circumstances of the Yemenites is in order. For reasons explained later in this introductory essay, most of the Yemenites arrived in Israel stripped of everything and, in addition, had to realize that almost all the occupations pursued by them in Yemen were useless in the new country. This created the impression that all of them had been very poor back in Yemen, while in Israel dexterity, industry, and thriftiness enabled many of them to work their way up. This impression is only partly true. Yemen is a good, fertile country. Even prior to the exodus, after hundreds of years of devastating anarchy, oppression, and cataclysmic famines, many Yemenite Jews enjoyed some degree of prosperity (see page 59). In the High Middle Ages, the tenth through the twelfth centuries, we invariably find the Yemenites as donors, never as receivers.

The first document relating to Yemenite Jews was a collection of letters by a Babylonian *gaon* to a large number of Jewish settlements in Yemen, praising them for contributions made earlier and eliciting further gifts. Yemenite charity was strictly organized with fixed quotas assigned to each congregation, public vows to be made on holidays, and personal donations on special occasions. In each locality the *gaon* had official representatives, often known to him either personally or through previous correspondence. No donations or legal questions were to be sent to the yeshiva directly. All contacts had to be made solely through the high court in the capital, appointed by the *gaon*.

These letters, which were collected and preserved, perhaps because of their beautiful Hebrew style, were written around the middle of the tenth century. At the end of the twelfth century Moses Maimonides wrote his famous epistle to the Yemenites and opened it with a profuse praise of their charity, hospitality, helpfulness, and munificence, renowned throughout the Jewish communities from Spain to the end of the world. As long as it had been commonly assumed that the Yemenites always had been wretchedly poor, these opening words of Maimonides' epistle were regarded merely as polite phrases. Fortunately, however, the

Geniza has preserved an elaborate document from Yemen detailing such a large gift for Maimonides that it must be understood as a donation not for him personally but for his *midrash,* or school. The Geniza contains also very extended letters of thanks sent by Jewish dignitaries in Old Cairo to maecenases in Yemen, and when Yemenites began to settle in Egypt, we find their names in communal lists among the contributors to public appeals and not as beneficiaries of public charity. Finally, when Jerusalem was repopulated by Jews after its conquest by Saladin in 1187, one of the three synagogues founded there was called the synagogue of the Yemenite. We have letters from the pen of this man. It is evident that the synagogue bore his name because he had made the main contribution toward its foundation.

Maimonides' epistle to the Yemenites was a sign of the times. The comparatively tolerant High Middle Ages were drawing to their end. Maimonides himself had escaped with difficulty the disastrous persecutions by the Almohads, who almost liquidated the once flourishing Jewish communities of Morocco and Spain. The incessant wars between Crusaders and Muslims kindled religious fanaticism everywhere, but also generated messianic and chiliastic expectations. These were by no means confined to Jews nor, within the Jewish community, to those of Yemen. In Iraq four such movements have been noted in the twelfth century alone. But in Yemen a particular religious situation prevailed. The country seethed with Muslim sectarianism, expressed partly in esoteric refinement and partly in stark fanaticism. Both affected the spiritual and physical existence of the Jews.

In a book written in the early 1160's, Nethanel ben
Fayyumi, then leader of the Jews of inland Yemen,
explains that Mohammed was a true prophet and the
Koran a book revealed by God, for there was constant
emanation from the world of holiness to the world of
matter in order to save it from Hell. Religion was like a
medicine adapted by God to each nation according to
its state and needs; naturally Islam was not destined
for the Jews, who had been chosen by God for his
special message—as the Koran itself repeatedly says—
moreover, they were not chosen because of their own
merits but by God's grace. This statement, profusely
illustrated by quotations from the Bible, the Talmud,
and the Koran, forms only a small part in a philosophical theory of emanation from the spiritual world to the
world of matter. Such reasoning probably was satis-
factory for the intellectuals from both camps but not
for the Jewish masses and the Muslim fanatics. The
latter demanded outright conversion to Islam, and the
former began to ponder, why should they suffer so
much as Jews if the other religion also was given by
God; or, perhaps their tribulations were an indication
that the time of the Messiah was at hand. Soon, both a
leader to apostasy and an alleged Messiah made their
appearance.

Meanwhile, Nethanel had died and his son Jacob had
taken over the leadership of the Jews in the highland
of Yemen. In the triple calamity of forced conversions
in the provinces conquered by the fanatics, of
apostasy, and messianic troubles, he applied to Moses
Maimonides, the recently (1171) elected head of the
Egyptian Jews. Jacob had addressed Maimonides in
elaborate Hebrew, and Maimonides, as was his habit,

retorted in kind, but soon he passed over to simple and straightforward Arabic. For, as he repeatedly emphasized, he wished that his letter (or rather letters) should be read out to women and children in order to strengthen their faith. He uses very harsh words about Christianity and, especially, Islam. Without referring, of course, to the simile used in the book of Jacob's father, he likens the other religions to fake images made of stone as contrasted with the living human body.

To us it seems strange that the princely philosopher Maimonides who lived in the center of the Muslim world, and moreover, was a close friend of leading Muslim dignitaries of Egypt, should write in such a vein, while an obscure man in faraway Yemen, like Nethanel ben Fayyumi, should defend an attitude seemingly so humane and modern. The difference lay in the basic philosophical concepts, the aims pursued, and the audiences addressed. In his attitude to the sister religions Maimonides did not differ from St. Augustine or Thomas Aquinas or any of the great teachers of Islam. Anyhow, Maimonides immediately was acknowledged by Yemenite Jewry as the leading religious authority. The ink had hardly dried on the fourteen volumes of his code of Jewish law, when three copies were ordered from Yemen, probably one by each of the three centers of Jewish scholarship in the country: Aden, Sanaa, and Sa'da.

But the tribulations of the Yemenite Jews had not yet come to an end. Saladin had taken possession of Egypt in 1171 and, a few years later, sent one of his brothers to conquer Yemen. This conquest, which was

a longdrawn affair, must have brought momentary
reflief to the Jews, for the Ayyubids, the dynasty
founded by Saladin, were orthodox Muslims, and
orthodox Islam is opposed to forced conversion. But in
1196 a nephew of Saladin, a half-insane person,
became ruler of the country and, among other
unorthodox actions, left the Jews the choice between
Islam and the sword. He did so perhaps in order to
strengthen his shaky position. In those days the
community was lead by a man called Madmun-
Shemaryahu ben David, probably a descendant of the
first Madmun spoken of above. All the Jews of inland
Yemen openly converted, and finally Madmun, who
had tried in vain to intercede for them, led the
Adenese Jews into Islam. We possess a Geniza letter
indicating the exact day and hour of the event and
adding that some particularly religious persons who
returned to the Jewish religion were beheaded.

But Madmun proved to be farsighted. As he himself
reports in a letter written in July, 1202, the tyrant was
murdered by his own troops (a fact known also from
Muslim sources); all the Jews, both in inland Yemen
and in Aden, were permitted to return openly to their
religion and the Shavuot holidays were celebrated in
great joy. When local Jew-baiters tried to make
trouble, they were suppressed by the authorities. The
turn of events is ascribed to the interventions of Jewish
notables in Cairo, headed, of course, by Moses
Maimonides.

This letter was sent in two copies via North Arabia,
a country out of bounds to non-Muslims. It was carried
by special messengers or by Muslim business friends of

Madmun. In a legal document, written in Old Cairo at the time of Abraham, the son and successor of Moses Maimonides, a large sum forming the estate of a merchant drowned in the Indian ocean was attested as forwarded by Madmun with a Muslim judge, who also engaged in trade. At that time, Jewish travelers from Aden to India were not any longer as frequent as they had been before; a loosely organized, but powerful hanse of Muslim merchants began to acquire almost exclusive control of the trade with India and the Far East. Yet we possess comprehensive *responsa,* or legal opinions, sent by Abraham Maimonides, as well as by his great-grandson Joshua to the scholars of Aden and inland Yemen. And despite the decline of Jewish trade and travel, the traffic in books increased rather than diminished.

In the letter describing the events of the year 1202, Madmun-Shemaryahu orders from Egypt copies of Maimonides' medical work and asks the recipient to buy for him any other fine books he could lay his hands on. The copy of the *Tahkemoni,* the chef d'oeuvre of the Spanish Hebrew poet Judah al-Harizi, presently preserved in the Bodleian Library, Oxford, bears a dedication to "Shemaryahu, the Prince of the Land of Yemen." No doubt, the poet, while passing through Egypt in 1216 or so, heard about the Adenese bibliophile (who is known also as a patron of scholars from a Geniza letter) and sent him this copy in the hope of rich reward. The *Tahkemoni,* a kind of a collection of short stories in rhyming prose, largely autobiographical and full of puns and allusive phrases, became extremely popular in Yemen and was repeatedly imitated. Its Bodleian copy is an example of the loving care with which the Yemenites preserved books throughout the centuries. It is no exaggeration to say that many of the valuable manuscripts of classical Hebrew literature preserved today in the libraries of Europe and the United States have come originally from Yemen, where they had been acquired thanks to the zeal for study and love of poetry of the medieval Yemenites and also thanks to the modest prosperity which they enjoyed.

The endeavor to be in touch with new developments in the main centers of Jewish creativity did not induce the Yemenites to neglect the advancement of their own age-old traditions. The study of the Talmud, so characteristic for the East-European *shtetl*, was not popular in Yemen; it was left (as originally designed) to a few select scholars. The Yemenites meticulously studied the Bible and the Mishna, the post-biblical Hebrew code; consequently, they have preserved an exact knowledge of the readings, especially of the Mishna, lost to the Jews of Europe. The commentary on the Mishna by Solomon Adani, who was brought as a child from Sanaa to Hebron in the Holy Land but lived in the Yemenite tradition, probably is the most important traditional work of its kind ever written.

Secondly, the Yemenites avidly collected Midrashim, that is, moralizing, well-worded, even witty homilies on the Holy Scriptures. The late Middle Ages was the great period of the Yemenite Midrash anthologies, which are worthy literary compilations in themselves and priceless for the history of Hebrew language and literature, since they contain many ancient elements not preserved elsewhere.

Thirdly, Spanish, and later also Italian, Hebrew poetry was greatly admired by Yemenite Jews and much copied and imitated. This activity culminated in a large poetical creation in the style of Judah al-Harizi's *Tahkemoni,* forty-five pieces in rhyming prose, often interspersed with long poems, written by Zekharyah al-Zahiri of Sanaa in the years 1568–80. His book is even more autobiographical than al-Harizi's since it is strung on two main themes: the author's extraordinarily extended travels and the sufferings which the Jews of Yemen had to endure in his time. Zekharyah traveled to India, Iran, Turkey, Syria, and Palestine, where he visited practically every place of significance and listened to all the great men adorning the schools of the country at that time. Finally, he returned via Egypt and Ethiopia back to Yemen. He visited the Holy Land a second time but was unable to fulfill his vow to settle there.

The tribulations of the Yemenite Jews were caused partly by the tyrannical character of the ruling Imam and partly by the attacks of the Ottoman Turks, who began to conquer Yemen, opening with this a long era of upheavals which came to an end only in the course of World War I. The Imam put the Jews of Sanaa and other places into labor camps for a full six years, pillaging their property and providing them with next to no food. It was during these years of utmost privation that Zekharyah wrote the major part of his book, which is so full of wit, invention, and verbal artistry. Clearly he conceived the book in order to lift up his own spirit and that of his fellow prisoners during those pitiful years.

For the modern reader, Yemenites included, Zekharyah's *Sefer Ha-Musar* probably is the most interesting Hebrew book written in Yemen. But at the time of its writing it did not become very popular. The stern, pietistic, and mystical mood of the period did not approve of a book given to mere entertainment. All poetry, including that destined as a pastime in the long weeks of wedding celebrations and other festivities, had to be religious. A specific type of Yemenite poetry developed and became so widely accepted that there is hardly a Yemenite house without one or several books of songs, which became as ubiquitous indeed as Bibles and prayer books.

This particularly Yemenite type of poetry seems to have originated in the lower hill country, where it had been habitual to indicate in the diwans, or collections of poems, according to which melody the individual poems should be sung and which dancing pace should accompany their recitation. For a poem, albeit often rather long, as a rule, was intended to be sung, and certain types of poetry, the most popular ones, had to be enacted in dancing by two, sometimes three, old men. The agility, gracefulness, and perseverance of these aged dancers (I had opportunity to observe different ones over forty years and more) are astounding. Old men (and not young women, of course) are the performers, for the poems have a mystical undertone, and who is more aware of the mysteries of life than those who are on the threshold of death? But these dances also contain elements of playfulness and trickery, of catching and escaping, and some other traits, which might become more intelligible to the uninitiated once the folklife of the Muslims of Yemen will become better known.

These poems were written in Hebrew, Aramaic, or Arabic, or in a mixture of two of these languages, that is, one stanza in Hebrew, the second in Arabic, the third again in Hebrew, and so forth. The Yemenites were fluent in Aramaic (the language spoken by the Jews after they had given up Hebrew and before they adopted Arabic), for every Sabbath the weekly lections from the Five Books of Moses and the Prophets were read out in the Yemenite synagogues both in Hebrew and in the ancient Aramaic translations. (In some Yemenite synagogues in Israel this strange custom is still observed.) The Aramaic translation usually is read with breathtaking speed by a little boy, who knows it by heart, which explains the knowledge of this language among the Yemenites. There was another reason for its popularity. The heyday of Yemenite poetry was the seventeenth century, the time when the Kabbalah and its corollary, messianic expectations, dominated Jewish life. The Zohar and other classics of the Kabbalah are written in Aramaic. Thus, the Aramaic garb of a poem enhanced its mystical character.

A problem is posed also by the frequency of poems either totally or partially in Arabic. The great Spanish Hebrew poets, who possessed a complete mastery of classical Arabic, never used that language in their poetical creations, not even the secular ones. The employment of Arabic by the Yemenite poets may be compared to that of Yiddish by the teachers of Hasidism in eastern Europe. By the use of a language near to every-day speech both wished to be understood by the common people and to communicate with God on intimate terms.

The most prominent poet of the seventeenth century, and indeed the poet laureate of the Yemenites up to the present day, is Salim (Shalom) Shebezi, whose tomb near Ta'izz, the capital of southern Yemen, became a holy place and site of a popular pilgrimage (see page 122). The strength of the expression of his yearning after God and Zion, his longing for spiritual and physical redemption, the depth of his despair and the joy of his faith—all expressed in his dancing verse, betray him as a gifted poet who rightly deserved his popularity. Slightly over six hundred of his poems have been preserved, which, according to his compatriots, is only a small fraction of his output. According to Yehuda Ratzaby, the excellent expert on the subject, the total of traditional poems contained in the Yemenite song books is about 1,800.

Salim Shebezi witnessed and bemoaned the greatest of the many disasters that befell the Yemenite Jews in the seventeenth century: their expulsion from their ancient homesteads in the mountains and hills of Yemen to the fever-ridden hell of the shores of the Red Sea, where two-thirds of them perished. This event did not happen all at once, which is why different dates are traditionally given for it (see page 120). But recent research has proved that "the exile to Mauza" mainly took place in 1679. It comprised mostly the Jews of the highland and these, too, were called back after two years. But they were not permitted to return to their ancient synagogues, good houses, and old possessions inside the cities and villages. Everywhere they had to build suburbs of modest appearance and poor protection with the result that, whenever a war or a revolt menaced a town, the Jews were the first to suffer. Moreover, the chasm between the Muslims and the "protected minority" became ever deeper. The last two hundred and seventy years of the Jews in Yemen probably were the worst ones. Neither were these happy times for the Muslims.

How, then, did the Yemenites manage to overcome such wretched conditions and steadfastly cling to the faith of their fathers despite their great dispersion in over one thousand small communities? First, their socio-economic function has to be considered. In a predominantly agricultural society the Jewish craftsman provided all the services without which a farmer was helpless. The Jew was hated and despised as a member of another religion, but he was sought after and honored as an *usta* ("master," the title with which a Jew was normally addressed). The blacksmith made the ploughs, hoes, spades, and all the other tools the peasant needed in his daily work (see page 59); the coppersmith, his cauldrons and the implements of the kitchen, which are manufactured today from a great variety of other materials. Jewish villages consisting almost exclusively of potters were found wherever there was good earth in Yemen, and each village had its speciality for which it was renowned far beyond the confines of its district.

The most highly esteemed and most widely prac-
ticed Jewish craft was that of the gold- and silversmith.
Every Muslim was a warrior; his pride was his dagger
and his sword, and he wanted to have their hilts and
sheaths artistically ornamented with fine silverwork.
The Muslim woman was an ambulant savings account;
she wore her riches on her body in the shape of
exquisite jewelry fabricated by the ubiquitous Jewish
silversmith. The Jewish townswomen, too, made high
demands on his art. Some ornaments brought by them
to Israel, especially in the course of earlier immi-
grations (starting in 1882) easily compete with the best
examples of jewelry produced anywhere in the world.
A comprehensive study on this subject is still
outstanding.

Silversmithing attracted the learned Yemenite Jew
because it enabled him to study while working. The
sacred texts were either known by heart or a boy
would read them out while the working adults would
discuss them. Zekharyah al-Zahiri, whose poetical
creation has been described above and who was also an
accomplished Talmudic scholar, earned his livelihood
as a silversmith. Rabbi Joseph Qafeh, today the
Yemenite member of the rabbinical high court of the
State of Israel and the learned author of fifteen or so
volumes, was trained as a silversmith and exercised that
profession in his youth.

The art of weaving occupied a similar position. It
engaged the hands and the feet of the craftsman but
not his mouth. In the Middle East in general the
weaver's profession was despised; the situation in
Yemen was different, probably because there he often

worked directly for the customer. Some of the most famous Yemenites, such as Salim Shebezi, the poet, or Shalom Shar'abi, the Kabbalist, were weavers. The beautiful legend on page 127 shows the high opinion the weavers themselves had of their work. A Jewish village in southern Yemen inhabited almost entirely by weavers has been studied and described by me in detail. (See "For Further Reading.")

A man called "a tailor" in Yemen did little cutting and sewing but mainly embroidery. The cut of the local attire was simple, but both the festive robes of the men and all female clothing, especially the trousers from the knees downward, were richly embroidered. (In Yemen men did not wear trousers; therefore saying of a man "he wears trousers" means he behaves like a woman.) This occupation, for the same reason as silversmithing and weaving, was cherished by scholars. On the other end of the Muslim world, at Fez, Morocco, the students of the famous Qarawiyin mosque and college used to earn their livelihood by embroidering women's trousers; one sees that similar socio-economic conditions create similar results. In the 1920's, I remember, Yemenite men in Palestine still were the finest embroiderers. Nowadays, of course, no one has any more time for such a delicate art.

Leatherwork was another and most ramified craft. Yemenite agriculture was largely based on irrigation, and this was done with leather buckets, manufactured and kept in repair by the Jew (see page 53). He also produced the various knapsacks and bags used in the country and he was the furrier, who worked goat- and sheepskins into different types of coats, with or without sleeves. Leatherwork, however, seems not to have given rise to a decorative art. Basketweaving, on the other hand, developed lovely patterns, successfully imitated in Israel.

Altogether I have noted about seventy arts and crafts exercised by the Jews in Yemen, some of them, in accordance with the then completely underdeveloped nature of the country's economy, of a very primitive character. In a two-volume book on Yemen, published in 1936, the Muslim author writes that all the handicrafts in the country were in the hands of the Jews. This was a gross exaggeration, but it reflects the impression made on the visitor.

Was, then, the mass emigration of 1949–50 a loss to the country and damaging to the emigrants themselves? Not as much as the preceding pages would suggest. For the specific socio-economic role of the Jews in Yemen was drawing to its end and they were caught in the dangerous process of being thrown out from the changing economy of the country. Cheap European trinkets and fabrics were already seen on the markets of Sanaa by the end of the nineteenth century. After World War I the country was swamped by Italian, Japanese, and Russian goods. The quality Jewish craftsmen gradually became redundant in so far as natural catastrophies and persecutions had left any. Sémach, the meritorious emissary of the Alliance Israélite Universelle of Paris, writes in 1910 that of 107 weavers he had found in Sanaa six years before, after the terrible wars and famines only seven had remained.

Moreover, the murder of Imam Yahya in spring, 1948, showed the Yemenites that the old order of things was coming to an end. The Zaidi Islamic law, under which they lived, was humiliating and oppressive; but it was law, and the Yemenites, the students of Jewish law, had an understanding for it. Modern nationalism, as the bloody events in Aden (then still under British rule) proved, was lawlessness; it permitted any crime against a minority—as long as it was unable to fight back. The Jews left the country at the right time. It simply meant saving their souls.

No doubt, the exodus involved great material losses. The houses, and, in the country, fields and cattle, had to be sold for next to nothing, if they could be sold at all. Immigrants brought with them hundreds of deeds of property, because they were unable to sell. Much or most of the money and other valuables they took with them had to be given as ransom or tribute or "customs" in the unruly districts they had to cross. In the modern economy of Israel, practically no occupation exercised by them in Yemen had any value. The *usta,* the "master," became an unskilled laborer. Naturally, for many this was a great tragedy. But in Yemen, too, they would have been forced to look for new occupations, and there they could not have found the guidance, encouragement, and variegated opportunities provided to them in Israel. As I was able to observe in the early 1950's, the older people found consolation in their faith and the privilege of living in the Holy Land, while the younger ones wholeheartedly plunged into the occupational reshuffle.

Finally, a word about the spiritual upheaval engendered by the emigration. There can be no doubt that the specific spirituality of the Yemenites was furthered through the tradition-bound society of their native country. The Zaidi sect, which ruled Yemen, had high regard for religious study. Learnedness was an indispensable quality required from the Imam, its ruler. But the majority of the rural population was illiterate, while the Jews living among it had mastered the art of reading. This gave the Jews self-confidence and the conviction that they were on the right path; their life conformed with the recognized cultural values of the country.

This situation accounted also for the social attitudes of the Jewish women and the absence of a chasm or tension between their own secular peasant culture with its popular songs, jokes, and stories, and the book culture of the men, centered in the synagogue. (In the villages women usually did not attend public services and did not know any Hebrew prayers. Once I asked a little immigrant girl, "Does your mother pray?" "Certainly," she answered, "but she says to God what she wants, not what is written in the books.") Seeing their husbands and sons held in awe by the illiterate environment, the women proudly identified themselves with the Jewish book culture, although they had no share in it. In simple families one could easily observe that the mother was eager, at least as much as the father, that her son should learn what was proper to know.

Yemen's traditional world is in jeopardy. The People's Democratic Republic of (Southern) Yemen has gone Marxist; The Republic of (Northern) Yemen is an uneasy compromise between republicans and royalists. Both states are fiercely nationalistic. Had the

Jews remained in Yemen and stayed alive, they would have been thrown out of their age-old spiritual world in the same measure as they already had been in the process of losing their socio-economic function in the country. But, as the example of all other Arab countries shows, they would not have found opportunities for a life the like of which they were offered so richly in Israel.

The stories and legends collected in this little book depict the Jew in Yemen, not the Yemenite in Israel, who is quite a different person. Yet the memories from the old country are cherished and kept alive. Learned Yemenites are contributing much to their conservation in writing. At festive occasions, traditional attire and jewelry, song and dance are displayed. And most important: the imponderable influence of the old life is felt in many ways, comparable to the imprint made by the East-European *shtetl* on the life of large sections of American Jewry. Thus, the world presented here, remote as it is in every respect, does not lack after all a certain amount of actuality.

LIFE

A Good-for-Nothing and the Power of Destiny

Old Oded was a man of integrity. He did not talk about people, and people had nothing to say about him. He was not clever, but everyone respected him.

But his son, Ibn Oded, is a good-for-nothing. Although he is not yet twenty, he is already quite fat and gross, while in our country people are usually slim and lean; he is greedy beyond any comparison, and wears two or three shirts and as many or more coats and overcoats, and why? Because in every article of clothing we have pockets in which almonds and raisins and all manner of sweets can be carried, so that we have something to nibble when we are hungry or bored. His upper and lower pockets are always full, but that is not enough: when he meets someone in the street the first thing he does is to put his fat hand into the other's pocket and take out whatever is in it. He seems as simple as a child. On the Sabbath, when he comes out of the synagogue with the boys, they tear, pinch, and push him, and also sometimes knock him against a girl—which is by no means proper—but he only laughs at it. But he is not really stupid, and sometimes is quite cunning. Of course, he still can't read the Torah properly. We don't have a reader who reads the Torah to us, but everybody who is called up has to do it himself, and woe to him if he puts a vowel or accent in the wrong place. Ibn Oded still has to practice his portion weeks beforehand with the schoolmaster. When it is his turn at last, he upsets the whole litany and it is pure blasphemy.

But, worst of all, he runs after the women so. In the afternoon, when all the people go to pray in the synagogue, he sits by the road down which the women must go to the wells to draw water, and stares at them. First he happened to stare at one whom we call the girl of the "holy"; "holy" means the community house where, for instance, the children's school is, and the community chest, and in general everything that belongs not to one but to all in common; and so— as it were—does she. Her father in the time of the Turks was a purveyor to the army, the smart officers went in and out of the house; first she was seduced, then she did it with pleasure, and in the end she drank medicine to become barren, and now she would not even reject a leper. Her brothers are good lads and each time she causes a scandal, they are at their wits' end and mourn as though a son had died. First Ibn Oded kept company with that girl, and it lasted for quite a time. Then he fell in love so violently with a woman who is now my wife, a girl from the house of my cousin Sa'adya, that he determined immediately to marry her and asked his father to woo her for him. He did what was necessary, but got a hint that the connection was not desired. Nevertheless, Ibn Oded did not give up his desire and the whole town knew that he wanted to marry the girl. This was not at all agreeable to the Sa'adyas, and one day someone came to me (of course not one of the brothers, that would be unsuitable), a cousin of hers, and proposed

to me that I should marry her. My father had died
when I was two, and, because it is a law with the
Imam that a Jewish child who has the misfortune to
lose his father is forcibly converted to Islam—for
Muslims think that their religion is the natural one
and the other religions merely a custom that a father
is allowed to hand on to his child, but which is an-
nulled by the death of the father—in order to escape
this fate I was seemingly adopted by my mother's
brother, and lived with my mother in his house, although we have a house from my father. For this reason the cousin who came to me with the proposal of
marriage thought that I should be especially willing
to accept it. But I thought that it is not right to marry
a woman with whom one has been brought up from
the first day in the same house; I thought also that
she was too closely related to me. This man did not
leave off until at last I said, "I'll leave the decision
to my mother. If she says 'yes,' I'll marry; if not,
not." Why my mother? Because she is with the girl
all day and knows her quality; but what do I know?
My mother decided thus: If Sa'adya (her brother)
says "yes" without any consideration, conditions, or
delay, then I should woo her; if not, not. So the same
evening I sent my father's brothers and their sons to
old Sa'adya. He thought this and that but in the end
it happened as my mother had stipulated; the mutual
obligations were fixed and we were betrothed. At first
it was kept a secret. Between betrothal and marriage
there always is a whole year, but in my case it was
two and a quarter years. Once the bride's mother was

ill, another time an aunt died, and as a matter of fact the Sa'adyas didn't after all really wish it, for they are rich and I am not.

Although the engagement was not official the whole town nevertheless knew about it next day and this was really our intention. Now you must know that Ibn Oded liked me—I cannot tell you how much—and also I liked him well enough. How can one like so unworthy a man? Well, it was predestined! Ibn Oded used to come and visit me, anyhow, quite often, but after my engagement he came to my shop every day and sat there for hours. Each day he asked about the engagement and each time I said I knew nothing about it. Eventually he began to make fun of me and it seemed that he had ill intentions.

One Friday I was sitting at the schoolmaster's to have my hair cut. Why, indeed, at the schoolmaster's? The schoolmaster teaches the children five days. On Thursday afternoons he gives the boys a trim, and Friday they have free, and then the people of the community come to him and have their hair cut. Isn't that highly irregular? Not at all. You are right insofar as the barber is very much despised by the Muslims; no Muslim would ever give his daughter to a barber or a barber-surgeon (who applies leeches) or a tanner. These only marry among themselves. If one Muslim calls another a barber, he can be haled into court. We Jews don't despise anyone for his profession; with us baths are heated by burning dried dung, not only cow dung, but also—by your leave—what is taken from outhouses (it is mixed with cow dung);

don't think that the people whose job this is are thought less of than anyone else, on that account. "Aristocracy" with us means only that someone is descended from an unsullied family and can support himself by his own work.

So now I sat at the schoolmaster's and my head was already wetted when suddenly Ibn Oded entered the house and at once called out, "Take me first!" Once before it had happened that the schoolmaster had taken a resident foreigner waiting in the line before a regular resident. The latter said nothing, but after a few days the schoolmaster received a summons before the Muslim court for insult and got three days' imprisonment. (We Yemenites are unfortunately the sort who, on the least pretext, will shout, "A lawsuit before the Sheik!" or, "To the lawcourt for judgment!") Ibn Oded, of course, only wanted to quarrel with me. Now I said very softly, "What, are you going to take a 'barber' first, then?" As soon as Ibn Oded heard that, he seized two or three people who were sitting there waiting to be shaved and shouted to them, "You are to be witness that he called me a 'barber.'" Since, as you already know, "barber" is a very strong swearword among Muslims, he could now denounce me before the Muslim lawcourt. The following Friday I got the summons to appear before the Sheik. With us, the Sheik is mayor; the smaller lawsuits are decided by him and larger ones come before the lawcourt of the Kadi; there is such a one in our town. Ibn Oded accused me on Friday morning, because that's when there is the most work to be done in the shop and so that damaged me most. I wanted to send an uncle as legal proxy, but Ibn Oded insisted that I come myself. Of course, I denied that I had said "barber," but it was no use, the Sheik condemned me to eight days' imprisonment, probably out of friendship for the wealthy Oded. "What!" I said. "Is this justice? I'll appeal to the Kadi and ask whether eight days are given for such a thing!" "All right," said the Sheik, "go to the Kadi." The Sheik, of course, is irritated if anyone appeals against him, and I was in no mood to spoil my relations with him. "I'd rather not go to the lawcourt of the Kadi, although I am innocent, but I will do honor to our Sheik, if he is in accord with me, and stay three days in prison." The Sheik agreed and wanted to have me led away, but I said, "Mohammed has taken the Sabbath under his protection, and I'll only go to prison tomorrow evening." Ibn Oded declared that he could not permit this. Now, the judgment takes place in the house of the Sheik. He sits in the middle and judges, and those of the better class who have nothing to do go there and sit down with a hookah and comment on what they think worth commenting on. When N.N., one of the very richest Muslims, heard Ibn Oded's objection, he got up and said, "I warrant for this man. Go home." Ibn Oded still wanted to say something, but the Sheik scolded him, "Son of a dog! N.N. has given his warranty and still you are not satisfied." And he sent us away. On the Sabbath I met Ibn Oded and he greeted me with the greatest cordiality and wanted to talk with me as usual. "Listen, you," he said, "I am going straight to the Sheik to ask him to release you from your punishment." "No, my friend," said I, "nothing will come of it. I should gladly sit three months in prison to have a reason to get angry and so be rid of you."

After the Sabbath was over I took blanket, cushion, mattress, and hookah and went into the prison. Four or five friends also went with me, each with his pipe, to keep me company. How so, in prison? Yes, of course; it is like that with us. And if you like—when, for instance, a fellah who is dirty and full of lice is imprisoned in the same room—you give the warder one and a half *bugshas*, that is, three *millim* (seven pennies) by our reckoning, and then he lets you sleep at his house. So I did on this occasion. "But come very early in the morning before people are about in the street." It was still half dark when I left the house next day, I had only prayed first. In this way I sat out my punishment and paid for my stay in prison. For every full day one pays a quarter of a *tuman* (seven pennies), and on release one *tuman* for the tax.

At first Ibn Oded was nowhere to be seen. One day my small cousin brought lunch into my shop. You must already know that there is, as very often in Yemen, a separate town for the Jews next to the Muslim town. This is called for short, "the town," and the other, "the village." Between the two is the market, and there I had my shop. When my little cousin, he was a Sa'adya, wanted to go out of the gate of the Jewish town with the dishes, he was detained by Ibn

Oded, who said, "Wait a moment, you. I'll pour something into the food that will make your cousin ever so strong!" What does such a child understand? In brief, the child held the dishes out and Ibn Oded mixed some poison into the flour pap. "But you must say nothing to him about it, or it will have no effect!" But scarcely had the little chap come in sight of me when he shouted, "Try the food, for Ibn Oded has poured something wonderful into it so that you may become strong." I had everything recounted to me exactly. Then I ordered him to pour the food out— yes, all the food, and to break the dishes. Sa'adya didn't know why and I told him nothing; then I borrowed some dishes from my neighbors that had not yet been cleaned and had the remains of food in them, and said to the little fellow, "There, now, run along home." Ibn Oded was already waiting for him at the gate of the Jewish town. "Well," he asked the little one, and looked very strangely, as the boy afterwards told me, "did your cousin eat it all up?" "Yes, everything," lied the little boy, "and it did him lots of good." "What, didn't he get sick, didn't he change color?" He was stupid, Ibn Oded. "No, not at all. Go and see for yourself." Ibn Oded could not refrain for long. Soon I saw him standing in the distance questioning a Kabyl who came out of the shop. (We call the fellaheen Kabyls, but they are all warriors, they are allowed to have all the arms they want and every one of them from childhood on carries a dagger in his girdle.) The Kabyl, who did not understand why he asked so excitedly about my health, laughed at him and went off. All day Ibn Oded hung around my shop. At last he lost patience and just when I wanted to close the shop and go to evening prayer he came in to me:

"Good evening."

"The same to you."

"How are you?"

"Thanks be to God, healthy and well."

"Are you not at all ill, not the least bit?"

"Not at all, praise be to God, I am as fit as a donkey."

"I believe you look ill, are you not sick after all?"

"On the contrary, since I brought some medicine home from Sanaa, I am doubly strong."

"What kind of medicine? Give me a little of it."

"No, my dear friend, it is much too expensive, besides I scarcely ever go to Sanaa, and I don't want it all finished."

From then on, Ibn Oded came constantly to my shop and my house to ask me, my customers, and my relatives about my state of health. When some weeks had passed and I still was in good health I appeared to him more wonderful and lovely than before, especially on account of the medicine from Sanaa.

Perhaps you have forgotten that Ibn Oded is an unrivaled glutton. You can be sure of getting good food at the Odeds', but this was not sufficient for him, and because he did not get more he went off after every meal to a woman (and a married one) who could cook well and liked to earn something on the side, and there he ate a second meal. Very early in the morning, at a time when other people are not yet eating, the woman had to cook him a fowl and other dishes, and he would eat it all up, the bones and broth included. I must however remark that he always ordered two meals: one for himself and one for the woman who is now my wife, the daughter of Sa'adya, whom he so badly wanted to marry. The housewife pretended to him that she took the meal to Sa'adya's daughter every time; and that she would therefore come to like him more and more, and finally would marry him because of it. But there wasn't a word of truth in it; the woman was only out for money. So it went on for a year or eighteen months. Suddenly he got to know, I don't know how, that it was all a pack of lies; besides, we had already once had a big flour-grinding for the wedding, only the death of the aunt had intervened. Ibn Oded took on against everyone, and especially against the deceiving woman, against me and my family (on my father's side, of course), and against my friend, Eliyoh Levi—who was also his friend—and decided to give us all one final blow.

On a Friday, very early in the morning—one rises early on Friday, in any case—he again ate as usual at the woman's house. Everyone was already at work; nobody was at home; only the woman was grinding what is necessary for the Sabbath down in the basement. Then Ibn Oded went up to the parlor (we have it on the second floor), opened the family cupboard (it is like a little room in the middle of the great parlor), opened the chest, rifled it of whatever he could, *gargushes*, books, and jewelry, and made off.

Gargushes are the costly girls' bonnets with gold and silver jewelry of all kinds on them; one of them can be worth as much as twenty English pounds; also, the books are much more precious with us than they are here, and especially Bibles in fine bindings, with Arabic and Aramaic translations, such as were among those which Ibn Oded stole. Where he took everything, you will soon hear, and he went off with his brothers into the villages to pay debts. The woman had meanwhile finished grinding and had gone up to the parlor in order to prepare everything for the Sabbath. There she saw the family cupboard open and the chest open, too, and everything in terrible disorder and the precious things stolen. Only Ibn Oded could have done that! Nobody else had been in the house. And she could easily think why! Immediately she ran to her uncle; he just said, "Hold your tongue and come with me to the Sheik." The Sheik listened to everything and said, "If you will promise me to hold your tongue and not to tell anyone, you will get your things back; if not, only bad luck will come your way. Ibn Oded is the son of important people, and he can't be hurt in the sight of everyone." She was satisfied with this and in the afternoon when Ibn Oded came back from the villages the servant of the Sheik was waiting for him at the gate of the Jewish town. Proudly carrying his head high, Ibn Oded went to the Sheik. I am a son of rich folk, what can happen to me! The Sheik spoke to him privately.

"You have stolen this and that from that woman."

"You are joking."

"I know where the things are."

"Then take them back to the victim of the robbery."

"If you don't confess immediately—and you are well aware that nothing will happen to you—if you don't confess, I will come tomorrow morning when the whole congregation is gathered in the synagogue for reading the Torah and call you a thief. Don't sully your father's honor."

Ibn Oded confessed and explained how it had all happened, and asked him not to ask for the things for a few days, because he wanted to play a trick with them. The Sheik agreed to this. This seems strange to you, but the Sheik is—it can't be helped—a son of a whore.

The next day, the afternoon of the Sabbath, the Sheik came with a great retinue, Ibn Oded among them, into the Jewish town to search for the stolen goods. He went straightway to my uncle's house and straight to the stables where the cakes of dry dung are kept; there is no window but only a round hole through which Ibn Oded had thrown one *gargush* and some volumes of a magnificent Bible. From there he went to the house of Eliyoh Levi, and from there to mine; everywhere stolen things were found. We were arrested and publicly examined.

"Who stole the things?"

My uncle, who is a fearless man, replied, "The Sheik."

"What, I, the Sheik? Do you want a thrashing?"

"If you want to beat me you can—you are the

Sheik. But because the Sheik knew where the stolen property was and we did not, it follows that he was the thief and not we." We were taken to prison, with chains on our feet this time. My uncle said, "This is too much, I am going to fight it out." The same day an accusation was made before the governor against Ibn Oded. The governor had been originally a servant of the ruler of our province. The ruler had been utterly devoted to the Imam; but at that time the Turks were ruling, and they had something against him and had exiled him together with his sons. They never came back to Yemen. The servant, however, took possession of all his master's property, paid tribute to the Imam and the Turks at the same time, and when the Imam became the ruler of Yemen, the servant became governor of our province. He married the Kadi's sister and the Sheik is hostile to him. The governor, the Kadi, the Sheik, and the noblest people in the town were gathered when Ibn Oded appeared to defend himself that evening. But instead of defending himself, when he saw the assembly before him, he told the whole truth from beginning to end. Well! That's just Ibn Oded. Meantime we were enjoying ourselves in prison in spite of our chains. Eliyoh Levi, an unrivaled wag, was in particularly good spirits. "Sidi Ali," he said to the warder (a Sayid, a descendant of Mohammed), "we have come to enjoy ourselves with you. Now take care that we get something out of it!" Not long afterwards the door opened and Ibn Oded was brought in, not in chains but in stocks. Do you think he was sad? Not at all. He took part in our jests all night long. What went on the next day and all that week in our town passes description. At last, after eight days, we were released and received compensation. But Ibn Oded got three months' imprisonment. He was not even allowed home on the Sabbath. In the end he had to give a present to the town; an ox was killed and the governor, the Kadi, the Sheik, and all the nobles ate it. The implication was this: You have sullied the town by your misdoing, we eat of the blood of your offering of atonement and thereby wipe it out. Ibn Oded never let himself be seen again at my house.

One day I was sitting in my shop; there was no one there; I had my left hand shading my eyes and was transferring various items from the slips into my ledger. Suddenly someone seized me by the neck with all his strength. I sprang up; it was Ibn Oded. He smiled very calmly at me and sat down opposite me, and without saying anything, he took the tube of my hookah from my hand and put it into his mouth. He wanted to talk but changed his mind; he didn't speak nor did I. A Kabyl came in to make a purchase and I gave him what he wanted and tied up his vessel with some gut. Suddenly the Kabyl said, "Allah curse your head!"

"And your beard! Why?"

"After all that wretch has done to you," glancing, with that, at Ibn Oded, "do you still keep up your friendship with him?" Of course, all the neighborhood knew what Ibn Oded had done.

"What sort of friendship? He comes to me against

my will; I throw nobody out; he might be a stone for all I care."

But the next day Eliyoh Levi, our mutual friend, came to me very quietly and said, "Do you mind if I talk to you about something?"

"Why should I? You can say anything you like."

At that he burst out, "Ibn Oded will give you any sum you care to ask if only you will resign your interest in Sa'adya's daughter." My face reddened. "Now you are angry after all!" he said. "Of course I am angry! Shame on you for saying such a thing. First, because of destiny. For she is betrothed to me and we have already been betrothed for two years. It is my destiny to marry her, and against fate one can do nothing. And in the second place, is a woman like cattle that she can be sold for money?"

I really had had enough. I sent my uncle and my cousins to the Sa'adyas and told them to celebrate the wedding forthwith, or nothing would come of it. First they were evasive and thought that the wedding could take place after Passover. "What," cried my uncle, "after Passover, when there is so much to do on the land? Then you surely will not be able to get it done." The Sa'adyas, of course, like so many Jewish families in our town, own large estates. In the end, the second week of the month of Adar was settled for the wedding week; we immediately began to grind corn and make other preparations quite openly, now that there was no further reason to keep anything secret.

As soon as Ibn Oded heard that I was being married, he was beside himself. Not only because of Sa'adya's daughter, but because we are of the same age, and because I, an orphan, without means, should have my wedding before the son of the rich Oded! He declared to his father that if I married in the second week of Adar, he must marry in the first. His father had to look for the bride. Now each week Eliyoh Levi would go to Damt on business, a place far distant from our town. There he saw the daughter of a silversmith who had also gone there from Sanaa. This man is a great master of his craft and every day he earns a Maria Theresa thaler—the real value is the same as a pound sterling in Palestine. But the money does not stay with him; what he earns by day, by night he gambles away. He can never begin to drink until he has three full mugs standing in front of him; then he gulps them down. It is said that he never gets drunk. His daughter is very beautiful, but was never much sought after as a match because of her father. This was just right for Oded. Levi once took a brother of Ibn Oded with him and he, too, liked her, and a week later the old Oded and his sons (of course without my Ibn Oded), went to ask for the bride. The old Oded had a choice meal prepared for him by a woman in Damt and took it to the house of the silversmith with the best wines in abundance. The silversmith ate and drank immoderately, but when old Oded began with his request, he said, "You think you can befuddle me with all your food and wine. Wife! Open the cupboard and show them that we need nothing and nobody."

"We came on your daughter's account."

"Greetings and welcome! Two hundred Maria Theresa thalers."

That was ten times the expected price of the bride. In the end, they agreed on a hundred, and the Odeds were to give riding beasts not only for the silversmith and his family from Damt, but also for all possible relatives from other towns; and the silversmith wanted a special house for himself, with all that went with it, for all the days of his stay in our town. The wedding was held in the first week of Adar. All the town was invited but nobody went; this is the way that we show a person what we think of him.

On the following Thursday evening my wedding took place. Nobody was missing from the whole community, not even the Odeds, although we had not gone to them.

Now it is the custom with us that the man who was last married takes the seat of honor next to the bridegroom: in my case, therefore, Ibn Oded. He came and brought wine, beef, and fowls' meat with him, and placed everything in front of him. My relatives found his presence highly embarrassing, but to go against precedent is of course impossible. My brother-in-law came and whispered in my ear, "Take care, he may try to bewitch you tonight or something worse. Don't talk to him and don't eat his food." I was very disconcerted. How could I not talk to Ibn Oded when he was of my own age and had the seat of honor next to me? Besides, I was very hot, the air was heavy with the breathing of two hundred people;

in addition, six great lamps were burning and the wedding costume was so heavy that I had to wipe my forehead constantly. Suddenly I began to cry—the tears flowed down, I wanted to keep them back but I could not. All the people started to look at me; my uncle came and shook me by the arm and said, "Well!" But nothing helped, I wept without ceasing. My mother's brother, the father of my bride, was furious, and said, "Look at the people—do you want to drive my guests away?" They led me out. I begged them to take some part of my wedding costume off, but that, as everyone said, was impossible. At last they calmed me and I returned to the festive chamber. There I had the idea of annoying Ibn Oded a little. Although I was in no mood for it, I ate and drank what was placed before me, but took none of his food.

For six months Ibn Oded loved his wife, and then he began to hate her; she was not allowed to go into his room any more, and when he met her there—for instance, when she gave him food and tidied up—he beat her and chased her out. She loved him very much, but he wished to have none of her.

Why all this? Because he still clung to the woman who is my wife. See how great the power of destiny is. His wife is far more lovely than she who is my wife, and is possessed of all the virtues, but he takes no pleasure in her because of the other.

Then I thought it was not right to be the cause of another's unhappiness and it occurred to me to do what so many in our town and in other towns of

Yemen have done, to emigrate to Palestine. So I left my native town with my mother and my wife—how that happened and about the journey itself I have already related.

This is, to tell the truth, the original reason for my emigration to Palestine, quite apart from the fact that it is, of course, the Holy Land and the land of freedom.

Protected Comrades

Because of the lack of a state authority, the majority of Yemenite Jews were dependent in many rural districts on the institution known as "protected comrades" for the security of their possessions and life. That is to say, a Jew, or a whole village of Jews, submit themselves by means of a solemn ritual of sacrifice to the protection of a powerful tribe, for whom it becomes a matter of the highest honor to administer justice in all circumstances to their protected comrades. The following stories—which are so chosen that the same man appears once on the side of the Jews and once on the opposite side—show how effective this institution can be.

Because of the Robbery of a Jew

The following happened to a Jew from Madid, who was the protected comrade of Ibn Mesar. The Jew came from Sanaa, the capital of the country, and was driving a donkey piled high with goods in front of him. He was overtaken and robbed when near his village. He warned the robbers, whom he knew well, "My protector is Ibn Mesar, he won't let you off scot-free if you rob me." But they did not listen to him, they beat him and took away all that he had.

Immediately the Jew ran off to Madid, shouting as he went, "Oh, help! Oh, shame!" until his protector and a crowd of people came to him and asked him why he was shouting. "Jaradi overtook me," said the Jew, "and robbed me, but I am under God's protection and yours." Ibn Mesar consoled him, "You will get everything back, to the last penny."

On the very same day Ibn Mesar collected five hundred armed peasants and made an assault on the Jaradi fortress. Two men fell on Ibn Mesar's side; Jaradi escaped and put himself under the protection of the tribe of Jabr. Ibn Mesar took the fortress and had it sacked; but the goods of the Jew which were found there were returned to him intact as they were.

Soon the Jabr tribe began hostilities against Ibn Mesar. Then the latter went into the tribe's territory and sacrificed several oxen on the grave of Jabr, the ancestor and patron of that tribe. The Jabr understood this and asked him, "Noblest of all sheiks, what do you desire?" Ibn Mesar made answer, "We are ready to leave our arms with you until you judge between us and the man who wronged us by robbing our protected comrade, because of whom two of our people have lost their lives."

Now, when the Jabr knew what was the situation of the man to whom they had given protection, they forced him to return home where he and his father were killed by the people of Ibn Mesar as retribution for his crime.

Quadruple Blood Money

Joseph Shukr was the protected comrade of the Bait Luhum, the most powerful tribe in the district. One day he came to a farmer to repair a bucket at his place. The buckets of the wells used for irrigation are made of leather and have to be continually mended. The mender is not always paid for his work, but he will come twice a year, after the winter and summer harvests, to the threshing floor, and there he receives a gift. Now while the Jew, Joseph, was sitting before the door of the farmer and mending the buckets, a half-witted Arab came up to him without the Jew realizing his intention, and struck him on the head with a piece of wood so violently that he fell down dead on the spot. The half-wit afterwards asserted that the Jew had bewitched him; he had, so to speak, been forced to murder him.

Now, whoever passed by the Jew's corpse, men, women, and children, raised a loud cry of "Shame, oh, shame!" The cry quickly spread through the whole village and into the nearby hamlets until in the evening of the same day two thousand armed farmers of the Bait Luhum tribe were ready for battle. But a roughly equal number had gathered to Ibn Mesar, who was advocate for the half-witted murderer. It would have resulted in a bloody battle if a certain family possessing judicial dignities had not interfered. "We are ready to hand over our guns if you will give us justice," the Bait Luhum declared, "but otherwise we will avenge our dead by kindling the torches of war, even if we all should perish by it." Both parties gave up their arms and the judicial family began its work. Ibn Mesar declared himself ready to render blood money at the rate that is paid for a Muslim—the half-witted murderer could not possibly be held responsible. The Bait Luhum were not satisfied with this, and demanded judgment by the noblest sheiks of the four great tribes of Yemen. With this the opposing party was satisfied; and the sheiks decided as follows: if the murderer had been in full possession of his faculties, the murder could only have been avenged with blood. But the advocate of the murderer must pay quadruple blood money: twice for the family of the murdered Jew and twice for the protector; and also the extremely high legal costs.

Ibn Mesar accepted the judgment and fulfilled everything required of him. Then the murder was reckoned as avenged, which the Muslims regarded as essential. For if the murder had remained unavenged, it is said, the murdered Jew would ride on the murderer on the day of the last judgment.

Muslims can forgive one another, but Allah himself takes care of the unprotected Jew's revenge.

The Sabbath Guard

The Arabic proverb, "If you are a Jew, be a Jew, and don't make a game of the Torah," has little meaning in Yemen, because there is seldom any transgression of the strict Jewish religious discipline there. Nevertheless, the following incident shows that the preservation of the Jewish law is also reckoned to be the affair of the Muslim community, and that self-seeking motives also naturally play their part.

If a Jew comes to the free farmers, the Gabili, and has prepared no food for the Sabbath, they give him everything necessary. But they do not sit down with him, or talk to him, as is usually their habit, for they believe that it is Jewish law that the Jew should shut himself off from the outside world completely on the Sabbath, and speak to nobody; and therefore no Gabili will disturb any Jew with business on the Sabbath.

The following occurrence is noteworthy. In the neighborhood of the main town, there lived a Jew who took the burden of the law somewhat lightly. In a year of drought and famine locusts came into the country in such vast numbers that the face of the sun was hidden and the air hummed with their swarming. The locusts are eaten by Muslims and Jews, and for many they are a favorite delicacy; since there was famine in the land everyone who could walk or stand set off in pursuit of them. The locusts came to the district of this particular Jew on a Friday evening. They are hunted at night and sometimes have to be followed a whole day's journey in order to be picked up by the sackful at dawn, when they are stiff and immobile from the cold of the night. The Jew set out and wandered after the locusts, although the other Jews in the village had already warned him against it. When the Gabili saw him, they called out, "Why do you come along here? Isn't it the Sabbath today, and how did you get the idea of going locust-hunting? You deserve to be killed for desecrating the Sabbath." They satisfied their feelings by beating him and taking away his sacks, and then led him bound before the Kadi. He put him in chains and allowed him to languish for a few months, then decided that the Jew's fields and house should be confiscated because of the desecration of the Sabbath, and banished him from the country.

Torah and Work

This description comes from the book *Even Sappir*, by Jacob Safir, who, commissioned by the Jerusalem Rabbinate, traveled from 1857 to 1863 in Egypt, Yemen, and India. His book is the most beautiful and original travel description in the Hebrew language.

This little town has a great rabbi. In Yemen the rabbi is called Mori. The Mori is judge, arbiter in questions of religious law, preacher, ritual slaughterer, cantor, and sexton, all in one person. And in spite of that, his office only earns him about one-third or one-quarter of the necessities of life. For that reason the Mori always has still another calling. This Mori, Joseph ben Sa'adya, is full of the Torah, of the fear of God, of wisdom and the knowledge of life. He has a wonderful knowledge of the Bible and its commentaries, and also of the Talmud, Maimonides, and up till the later codifiers, as well as of one of our greatest teachers in Poland. In addition, he is a thorough master of the Zohar, and he knows by heart every page of the writings of Rabbi Isaac Luria; on the whole, his memory is remarkable. He himself has written about the Kabbalah, and he also occupies himself with practical Kabbalah and astrology, makes amulets, prescribes medicines, and makes use of fortune-books; and also the non-Jews ask him for amulets and medicines (for he writes Arabic), and he is highly thought of by the authorities. In his dress he follows the customs of the country, so that men take him for a farmer or shepherd; by profession he is a blacksmith and makes arms, ploughs, spades, hammers, hoes, and in general all the tools which are used by the farmer. His workshop is a vaulted room on the slope of the hill on which the town is built. His old father and his younger brother, who are equally educated, help him in his work. The father looks after the bellows and holds the iron while the brother uses the hammer, and even during this hard work they talk of the Torah and other edifying things. Here in this vaulted room he makes rulings on religious law, judges and gives advice to all who desire it. Towards evening he takes his working tools and carries them on his back up to his house, then he goes to the synagogue and studies as is the custom here after the evening prayer. Even during the night he does not rest, but rather for him the night becomes a vigil of the Torah and of wisdom.

By virtue of the work of his hands he has also received blessings in this world. He owns a two-storied house with well-furnished rooms full of books and precious utensils, and the storerooms are well provided with wheat, barley, beans, lentils, raisins, wine, honey, cooking butter, coffee, nuts, and almonds. He has three wives, but only one son—by his third wife—called Joseph after him (this they only do after many children have died). The women grind corn, bake, cook, gather sticks in the fields, fetch water from the spring down in the valley, wash, dye, and also undertake all the necessary repairs to the house and the household utensils; and they do all this with the greatest cleanliness and purity and holiness. This is in truth what our wise men have said: "The Torah is good, combined with work." Hail to them in this world and the next!

Once I came into his smithy early in the morning. His father and his brother had not yet come; they do not live in the town but in a nearby village. A farmer was urging Mori Joseph to get his plough ready, as he had to go to work. So he called two of his wives, one worked the bellows and the other put on coal whilst she held a small child on her arm; he himself made the tools ready on the anvil. When I came into the vaulted room he greeted me with a friendly smile because he well knew that the picture which greeted me must have seemed strange. "Come, let me take this hammer and I'll help," I said. But he refused by remarking, laughingly, "Do you want to give up being a rabbi and become my workman?" I sighed deeply and said, "All hail to you, Mori Joseph, who are a smith, and alas for us who make the rabbinate a profession!"

How the Haidan Yemenites Went
to Palestine

Anyone who has come to know the Yemenites in Jerusalem and then comes into the Judean colonies, say, Rehovoth, will notice that he has a different type of people in physiognomy, clothing, and way of life, before him. These are the Jews from northern Yemen, known as Haidans. Nearly everything in this anthology comes from the Jews of the first sort, who have central Yemen for their home. The first emigration of the Haidans to Palestine, described in what follows, is of general significance because they were the pioneers in the change-over to agriculture among the Yemenites.

Although the Jews in our province suffer very little from oppression, their longing for Zion started to burn and became a great flame; and if outside circumstances had not prevented it, our whole district would have emptied itself of Jews. Nevertheless, it had not yet happened that two hundred and fifty people had departed from one place in Yemen to go to Palestine, as was now the case.

On the 12th of Tammuz, 5667 [1907], the caravan of emigrants left Haidan. We took with us all our household goods, and in addition twenty camels laden with coffee (which we thought to sell in Palestine). The farewell was heartbreaking, less for the Jews who hoped soon to follow us than for our Arab neighbors who knew that they would never see us again. The Arab women, especially, started wailing as they do when someone has died because they believed that we had certain foreknowledge that their land was destined to disaster, and that we were leaving because of this, whilst they, unprotected, would be abandoned to the terrible future.

On the third day of the journey we came to the desert, where it was possible to move only during the morning and evening hours. Here we were overtaken by blacks who wore only a loincloth. As is the custom in the desert, we had with us a man of the tribe of the district who was to act as guide for us and was supposed to guarantee our safety. But he had disappeared the previous night and had thus sold us over to the blacks. But we were armed with swords and six of us also had guns, so we awaited the attack fearlessly and in good order. As soon as the blacks saw this they did not dare to attack. Suddenly our guide reappeared, and now, after he saw that his cunning plan had gone astray, bade the blacks pass on. So we came into the coastal plain where the people, because of the fearful heat, live not in stone houses but in round, plaited huts. There we were detained for eight days until the ruler of that country gave us permission to proceed. At last, seventeen days after we had started, we reached the port of Midi. The whole company had made the journey on foot, only the women and the sick rode on camels. But to our disappointment we heard that a European steamer put into port only once in six months, so we had to hire two native sailing boats to take us to Aden. But since they had told us that we were not allowed to come to Aden carrying arms we sold our swords and guns; and just as we were going on board the boat, after five days' unbearable stay in the sultry heat ashore, a great horde of armed riders suddenly assaulted us. As we no longer had any arms we girded on the defenses of our forefathers: prayer and blowing the shofar. As soon as the attackers heard the sound of the shofar, they stopped because they had never heard anything like it and because in that country the Jews are believed to be great sorcerers. Two of our people went out to meet them and persuaded them to go away for a small sum of money.

All were glad when we at last went on board the boat. As it is said in the prayer book: A new song of celebration sang the redeemed on the shore of the sea. But our pleasure was short-lived, for on the second day, a Sabbath, a great storm arose, and for five days we literally saw hell open before us. The cold rain poured down into the undecked boats, the waves surged over them and washed the passengers this way and that. The storm unseated the mast of one of our sailing boats, and since the mast was set into the bottom of the vessel, the boat sprang a leak. Day and night we had to bale the water out of the boat and even the sailors lost their courage. In the midst of all this wailing, a woman bore a healthy girl, without difficulty, and we gave her the name of the boat; she is still living in good health at Rehovoth. When at last we arrived in Aden the doctor did not want to let us ashore because we looked like corpses after the sufferings of the journey and the sea voyage. But with the help of the famous millionaire Banin, of blessed memory, permission was given us at last and after seventeen days of quarantine, we were free to wait for a German steamer which took us happily to Jaffa, after a journey of three months.

However, the boat that was damaged during our journey had scarcely unloaded us and left the quay, when it turned turtle before our eyes and broke in two.

ENTERTAINMENT AND EDUCATION

A Fairy Tale and a Jest

These stories have nothing specifically Jewish about them, and the essence of the following story may also be found, for instance, in the Arabian Nights. They are one of the most important forms of entertainment, especially among the women, and are thus an essential element of the Yemenites' spiritual world.

The Story of the Manly Maiden or
Repentance Which Comes Too Late Is of No Use

Once upon a time, as they say, there was a man who had a wife as beautiful as the sun and as white as sugar, and the two loved each other dearly. By profession the man was a merchant, and one day he told his wife that he had to travel to a distant country to buy goods. Since they had neither children nor friends, nor dependents of any kind, his wife said to him, "How can you leave me here alone, since I have none to keep me company or to pass the time with me?" The merchant replied, "But what am I to do? I really have to go on the journey." She said, "Do you know what? Look around the market today, and perhaps you will find some pretty trifle there that will be just the thing to while away the time." The merchant went to the market and soon saw a dealer offering a goldfinch for sale; he was calling out, "This bird sells for a thousand dinars. Who buys it not shall regret it, and who buys it shall repent of it." The merchant went to him and asked him, "How am I to understand this, 'Who buys it not shall regret it, and who buys it shall repent of it'?" The dealer said,

"Just buy the bird and you will find out." So the merchant bought the goldfinch and took it to his wife and said to her, "This little bird, you know, eats only almonds and raisins, and drinks only milk and honey-water. Take care of it and enjoy it till I come home to you again."

The woman was enchanted, and forthwith began to prepare everything for her husband's journey. Soon the preparations were finished and the merchant kissed and embraced his wife and went out of the house, and she hastened to the upper story to watch him from the window.

Just as she leaned out of the window, however, the son of the Sultan passed by, and no sooner had he seen her than his passion was aroused, and becoming full of love's eager desire, he could only with great difficulty bring himself to return to his father's palace. There, before he could tell anything, he fell senseless to the ground, shivering, as though with a severe fever. All the doctors were summoned forthwith and the Sultan said to them, "Cure my son, the apple of my eye, my only one—for a hundred sons have I not." The doctors felt the prince all over and examined him but could discover nothing wrong with him. So the Sultan bade the doctors wait in the antechamber, and went into his son's room himself, hiding behind a curtain, for he hoped that the sick boy in his fever would say something to show what might cure his illness. And so it happened. The prince soon groaned and moaned and cried aloud, "Where are you, my love, where are you, my heart's delight?"

The Sultan now knew what ailed his son. He left the room and said to the doctors, "I know what is the matter with my son; you can go home." Then he called a wise old woman and said to her, "Go in to my son and cure him." The old woman spent the whole night in the prince's room, and before the sun had appeared through the rosettes of the window she knew that none other than the merchant's wife was the cause of his illness. The old woman went forthwith to the merchant's house and knocked on the door, calling out, "May I come in, my dear? My daughter is to be married today and she will not go to the ceremony unless you are there." The merchant's wife answered, "I cannot come, for I will not leave the house until my husband is safely returned from his journey." But the old woman would not give in, and finally the wife said she would come. She quickly went up to the upper story, washed and anointed herself, made up her eyes, painted her hands, arms, and feet, and attired herself, and was ready to go with the old woman.

As she went down the first step out of the house she stopped and turned back to the goldfinch, and said, "Dear little bird, goodbye." But it answered, "Good luck, my lady, you seem to have entirely forgotten me." "Why so, dear goldfinch?" said the woman. "Do you want something?" "No, dear lady, only I will tell you a story, if you will be patient and listen to it."

"With the greatest pleasure," said the merchant's wife, and the goldfinch began at once:

"Once upon a time, as they say, a boy and a girl who were cousins loved each other dearly. Their fathers were mortal enemies, however—for even with brothers such a thing sometimes happens—and so they could not show their love openly, and when they wanted to meet, they did so in secret, far away in the open fields. One day when they met, the girl complained, 'Dear soul, delight of my heart, what will be the end of this? I can't bear it with my family any longer. Because I love you, they would like to flay me alive. Today my father shut me up in the stables and turned the great lock to prevent my coming to you. But love made me so strong that I forced the door off its hinges and escaped. Tell me, what are we to do?' As soon as the young man heard what his cousin said, his passions were roused and he could scarcely contain himself for anger and grief. After a pause the girl said, 'Do you know what has come into my mind? Let us run away from here into a distant land. There we will be married and nobody shall hinder us.' The youth thought as she did, and so the two set out. Presently they came to the edge of the sea where they found a steamer about to sail. They took passage and went on board. Then it occurred to the girl that she had no provisions for the journey, so she quickly sent the youth to the market to buy whatever was necessary, repeatedly impressing on him the need to hurry and not to linger in the market lest—God forbid—he should miss the boat. Then, tired out by the stress of travel, she lay down in the boat on a bale of goods and fell asleep.

"Now when the youth came to the market of the foreign town and saw so many things which were new to him, he forgot the girl's warning and spent so much time in buying things and gaping that when he returned to the shore, the ship had already left the harbor. Overcome by grief and sorrow, he flung himself down and wept piteously, but his repentance came too late. Then the young man got up and wandered from place to place and from country to country, hoping to meet his cousin somewhere, and so he went ever on, until he came to a place thirty days' journey from that harbor, and there he said to himself, 'I will stay here until God shows me his will.'

"But the girl only awoke when the ship was already at sea. On seeing that the youth had not come back she cried and tore her hair, but no one paid any attention to her, until the captain came and asked her, 'What is the matter, girl?' 'Nothing,' she answered. 'But why are you crying?' persisted the captain, for he already liked the girl. Finally she told him everything that had happened to her. The captain comforted her and invited her to have a place in his cabin, and his wife received her in a friendly fashion, prepared a bed for her, and gave her food and drink. Thus three days went by.

"On the fourth day the captain's wife was promenading on the deck with their children and watching the passengers. When the captain saw that the girl had remained in the cabin alone, he hastened there and locked the door behind him, and tried with passion to bite her cheeks. But she gave him such a clout that his nose bled and the floor was drenched in blood. When the captain saw with what sort of person he had to deal, he began to say very softly, 'My dear, light of my eyes, I only wanted to show you that you have stolen my heart away and turned my head.' 'What else?' asked the girl. The captain did not realize that she was mocking him, and continued, 'Yes, I wanted to ask you to become my wife.' 'I will not be the wife of a man who has another wife,' answered the girl. 'Stop your chatter and take good care not to think about me again.'

"The captain had scarcely heard her words when he hurried on deck and, seizing his wife and children, threw them into the sea. Then he went down into the cabin, told the girl what had happened, and concluded, 'Now I am free to marry you and nothing stands in the way of your becoming my wife.' So you are that sort, thought the girl to herself; how true is the proverb which says: 'No reliance is to be placed upon men, they are worth even less than a louse.' But she pretended to be very friendly with him, saying, 'If you want to marry me, I am satisfied now, only you must wait until we come into harbor again so that we can celebrate the wedding in such a way as is fitting. Meanwhile, let us be friends.' The captain was delighted and walked about the ship with her, showing her everything there was to see, from the bridge to the stokehold; he explained to her how to get the ship under way and how to stop it, till she knew how just as well as he did himself.

"One day they came near a small island, and the

captain, to please the passengers, had the ship stop there for a few hours. The travelers, headed by the captain and the girl, disembarked and enjoyed being able to walk a little on dry land. When they got tired they sat down and ate and drank what they had brought with them. The girl brewed coffee, but put opium powder into the captain's cup. Scarcely had the captain drunk it when the opiate went to his head, and he fell down on the spot and lay senseless like one dead. The girl waited till there was no further visible sign of consciousness, then she hastened to the ship and had the sirens blown and the horn sounded. All the passengers who were walking on the island immediately gathered and went aboard. She gave the necessary orders to the Somalis[1] to get the ship under way. None of them ventured to refuse obedience to her, rather, they all agreed with pleasure to do whatever she bade them. She steered the ship by the correct course till she had brought all the passengers to their destination.

"Let us return to the captain. He lay senseless on that small island till the next day's sun beat on his face, when he sneezed vigorously and returned to his senses. He looked around, but nobody was to be seen, neither the girl, nor the passengers, nor the ship. Then he was sorry indeed for his wife and children whom he had criminally and uselessly done to death, as well as for the girl and the ship. But repentance which comes too late is of no use. Therefore, dear

---

[1] Most of the seamen on the coastal steamers of southern Arabia are Somalis.

lady," said the goldfinch, "if you go to this wedding you shall repent of it, just as that youth and that captain repented."

Then the woman said, "Yes, you are right, I would rather not go to the wedding." In short, she excused herself to the old woman by saying that she had a good deal of washing to do, and could not leave the house. But she certainly would go with her the next day. The old woman returned to the Sultan and told him all that had happened. But the prince still lay in a raging fever, taking neither food nor drink.

The following day the old woman again went to the merchant's wife, knocked at the door, and called out, "Now my dear, don't put it off any longer but come with me." "Gladly and with pleasure, dear Aunt," replied the merchant's wife, "but first let me dress, anoint myself, and make up my eyes." Now when she was going down the stairs of the house she stopped on the second step, turned to the goldfinch, and said to him, "Dear little bird, goodbye." But he said, "Good luck, my lady, have you forgotten me?" "Why," said the woman, "is there anything you lack, or do you want something from me?" "No, not the least thing," replied the goldfinch, "but just listen. Do you know what happened to the girl?" She said, "No." The goldfinch said, "Well then, wait a little and I will tell you.

"After the girl had brought the passengers to their destination, she had the steamer anchored in the harbor, and herself went ashore to see the town. As she was going through the market she saw Shachbender, the merchant prince. He at once went up to her and bade her welcome. Then he conducted her to his house, had coffee served, and inquired of her regarding her provenance and business. She told him about it in detail, how she was in love with her cousin and how she lost him, and that now she was in search of him. 'What has happened, has happened,' said Shachbender, the merchant prince, 'and since the Fates have brought you to our city, it has doubtless been decided by them that you should become my wife.'

"When the girl heard these words she thought in her heart, What the proverb says is indeed true, that who gets rid of a Muslim is brought low by God through an unbeliever. I had not hoped that God would save me from the hands of that captain, and now another man comes to me to persuade me to it. I should make a real mistake if I were to be unfaithful to my cousin—who, alas! even now is sitting somewhere bewailing me, I am sure—and married this vain peacock. But to keep up appearances she said, 'Good, noble merchant, I am ready and agreed, only first you must fulfil one condition for me. You must bring me forty young men and forty maidens, we will marry them first and then celebrate our own wedding.' Shachbender was satisfied with this and soon collected the forty couples. But the girl took the maidens secretly aside and dissuaded them with the plan that they all should run away together and set out into the wide world.

"On the next day, Shachbender and the forty

couples came on board the ship, where the weddings were to take place. The girl received them with great friendliness and had coffee served. Shachbender sat at her side and the young men had each his bride beside him. But she had told the server to put the opiate powder in the cups of the men, and very soon the draught did its work and the men sank senseless to the ground. When the girl saw that, she had the sailors put the sleeping men ashore and leave them there. She, however, went into the stokehold, got up steam, cranked the engine, and departed with the maidens.

"Some days later they came to a green island and there they all went ashore to drink fresh spring water and to enjoy themselves under the trees. Scarcely were they ashore on the island when of a sudden forty-one robbers appeared as though from the ground and, closing in on them, threatened them from all sides. 'Allah has delivered you to us!' cried the robbers, and prepared to fall upon them. But the girl called out to them, 'Greetings! honor and welcome! We desire nothing but to be agreeable to you. Since we have been at sea alone so long, we desire only to do you pleasure.' When the robbers heard these words the world seemed very bright to them and they were delighted. 'Then let us all go straight aboard,' they cried, 'and there make merry.' 'But why on the ship?' replied the girl. 'It is so beautiful here. First we should like to enjoy ourselves here and then all of you come on board with us.' After the robbers had agreed, she had coffee and candies brought from the ship by her companions. But she dealt with the robbers exactly as she had with the captain and Shachbender, and soon all the robbers lay there like corpses. Then she ordered her companions to strip the clothes from the sleeping men. The maidens did as she said, and soon the robbers lay naked as the day when they first saw the light, and they also stuck a radish in the behind of every man of them. But the girl and her companions put on the clothes of the robbers and now appeared as men. They boarded the ship, the girl cranked up the engine, and again they set off into the wide world.

"When the robbers regained consciousness the following morning, they found that they were as naked as the day when they first saw the light. Then they were sorry about their clothes and the girls and the ship. If you, my lady," said the goldfinch, "go to this wedding, you shall be as sorry as the robbers, and as Shachbender, the prince of merchants." "No, I will certainly not go," replied the wife, and she said to the old woman, "As I told you yesterday, I had a good deal of washing, and it is not all dry yet, so you must please excuse me for one more day. Tomorrow I will quite definitely come with you." The old woman growled angrily, but said no more and went her way.

Next day the old woman came early and bade the merchant's wife come with her. She quickly got ready and followed the old woman. Only when she was on the third step of the stairs of the house did she remember her goldfinch, and turned round to him to say goodbye. But he said, "You have indeed forgotten me." Then she was vexed, and said, "Curse you, and curse your procreator, and curse the man who brought you to me. Why are you always stopping me and why don't you let me go to the wedding like everyone else?" Then he said, "Do you know what happened afterwards to the girl?" She said, "No." He said, "Then wait a little while and I will tell you." The merchant's wife had absolutely no patience with waiting any more, but because she was so intrigued, she could do nothing else but sit down and listen to the goldfinch, who went on as follows:

"After the girl and her companions had put on the clothes of the robbers they sailed away into the wide world until they arrived at a port, where they brought the ship to anchor and went ashore. As they were coming to the town, they heard people mourning and wailing and saw a great crowd of people walking in the direction of the palace. When the girl asked what was the matter, they answered her, 'Our king has died and left no children. In such a case it is our custom, before the interment, for the queen to climb to the roof of the palace and to throw the crown down upon the crowd of men below. The man upon whose head the crown falls becomes king and he marries the widow of the dead king.' Hardly had the girl heard these words when she felt a violent blow on her head. She cried out, 'Oh! My head!' but instantly was surrounded by viziers and officers who lifted her shoulder-high and shouted, 'God bless our king!' The crown had in fact fallen on her head, and since she had men's clothing on, nobody knew that she was a girl.

"In short, the girl was brought to the palace in great splendor. The funeral service was held and the king taken to his grave. Then they set the girl upon the throne, brought her the books of accounts, and all the documents of the realm, and the keys of the treasure house; and a session of the senate was summoned before the new Sultan, and they drank coffee and were entertained till morning. And for the forty maidens who had come with her, she had special rooms made ready in the palace.

"But when the viziers saw that the new king was a beardless boy, they held it unseemly to marry him to the old widow queen. Rather, they agreed to give him for wife the daughter of the Grand Vizier, a very young girl of great beauty. Our girl, the Sultan, was not a little disturbed at the suggestion, but she thought, With time thought will come, and so she agreed to it all. The betrothal was celebrated immediately and the wedding took place eight days later.

"Now when the bride was brought to the Sultan her heart melted with passion at the beauty of her bridegroom. But he did not touch her or come near her, only played and jested with her till both of them fell asleep. Next morning the Grand Vizier came and asked his daughter how she felt. She wept and sobbed and told him all that had happened.

But the Grand Vizier said, 'Take care to let nothing be known of this. Such things happen. Only have patience till tonight.' The Sultan, when it was light, dressed herself in silk and satin and went into the audience chamber. There she gave judgment and received petitions, and issued orders and prohibitions until night fell.

"After the evening meal, the Grand Vizier's daughter was again brought to the bridal chamber. The Sultan, the girl, came to her and played and joked with her and thus half the night passed. And our girl began to think that matters had turned out well, as on the previous night. But when the daughter of the Grand Vizier saw that her burning desire was not satisfied, she burst into tears and would not stop sobbing and lamenting at the great wrong done her. Now when the girl saw that things could not go on like that, she spoke to the bride, revealing herself, 'You have breasts just as I have, there is no need to cry.' The bride could not believe her ears and so the girl opened her dress and the bride could doubt no longer. Then she became even more furious and wept for the cruel betrayal of which she was the victim. In order to comfort her, the girl began to tell her all that had befallen her: how she loved her cousin and fled with him from her parents' house, and how she lost him; and about the captain, and Shachbender, the merchant prince; and about the robbers; and how finally without her consent she was made Sultan. 'I am in your hands,' she said, 'it lies with you whether you betray me or whether you will keep my secret. But I will soon find a way for you.'

"Before the girl had finished she had won anew the love of the Grand Vizier's daughter, and when the tale was finished, she said to her, 'Light of my eyes, be calm, I will betray nothing. But to my father I must speak, for he is my father and I have nobody in the world but him, and I will implore him not to reveal your secret to anyone.' The girl was overjoyed at this answer and straightway called the youngest Somali who served as a sailor on the ship, made a cut in his little finger and let the blood drop on the bedclothes. He had to promise to hold his tongue on pain of death, then he was dismissed, but not without being handsomely rewarded.

"Now when the next morning the Grand Vizier heard from his daughter how things were with the Sultan, he beat his head against the wall and said, 'Vain fool that I am, I wanted to be the Sultan's father-in-law, and now I have nothing but shame!' But repentance which comes too late is of no use, and so he gave his daughter his oath to say nothing and to keep her secret.

"But the girl had the plaster-molder come and ordered him to make a portrait of her in plaster. Casts of it were to be put up at all markets and crossroads and places where there was a well. At every place a section of police was to be posted, with instructions to arrest anyone who wept or swore in front of the portrait, and to bring him before the Sultan. It was not long before the girl's cousin came across one of these portraits, and he recognized it as soon as he had seen it and immediately broke into loud lamentation, 'God knows who put up this portrait here, and only He, praised be He, knows where she can be at this moment, whose likeness it is.' Scarcely had he spoken when the police seized him and dragged him off to the Sultan's palace. His cousin, the Sultan, immediately recognized him, and was astounded at the change in fate that now brought him back again to her. She did not allow her joy to appear, but ordered the servants to bathe the prisoner, shave him, and put new clothing on him. Then she showed him to a roof arbor as beautiful as a jewel casket, and told him to await further instructions. The youth let everything take place, and waited in the arbor between hope and fear of what the Sultan might have in store for him.

"Next day the police were again at their posts, and lo! there came face to face with that portrait none other than the captain. As soon as he recognized whose portrait it was he began to swear terribly and tried to break it. He quickly received a blow on the head that felled him to the ground and when he came to himself he found that he was in the Sultan's palace. As soon as the girl saw him, she knew who he was and gave orders to hang him, which was done without delay. On the same day, Shachbender, the merchant prince, came face to face with one of the portraits. When he realized whom the portrait represented, he beat his breast and cried, saying, 'Ah! nobleman's daughter, would I knew where you were at this moment and what harm I have done you for you to play such an evil trick on me and my forty companions!' The police seized him forthwith and led him before the Sultan. She, the girl, said nothing, however, but let him wait until evening. Then she went to the apartment of the Grand Vizier's daughter and said to her, 'Do you know, I have got a splendid husband for you, none other than Shachbender the merchant prince, who is renowned in all lands.' But the Grand Vizier's daughter answered, 'I don't want Shachbender or any other. My life is bound to yours, and never again can I be parted from you. Yes, if your cousin were here I should be resolved to marry him after you, but only if it seemed right to you.'

"When the girl heard this answer she was very pleased. Then she called her forty companions together and said to them, 'Did you know that Shachbender has arrived at the court? Now you can all go back together to your homes and be married to your betrothed.' The maidens answered, however, with one voice, 'We will never be separated from you. If our betrothed come here then we will gladly be married, but never will we depart from here.'

"After these consultations, the girl finally had Shachbender called and when she had imposed on him a thousand dire oaths not to betray to anyone in that country what she would reveal, she told him everything that had happened to her since the day she left him, and notably that she had found her cousin again. Shachbender could make no end of praising God and his all-seeing wisdom, and said at last, 'Now then I must take the forty maidens with me, for their relatives are already preparing the fires of hell for me, because of this little business.' The girl, however, told him of the maidens' answer, so Shachbender went back to his country to fetch the young men. However, the relatives of the maidens would not permit their daughters to be married in some foreign country, and said to him, 'Much better that they should not be married than that we should leave them in a foreign land.' Then Shachbender let them see that the Sultan of that land would keep the maidens by force, if the young men did not come there and marry them. When the relatives of the forty couples saw this, they finally gave their assent. So the fathers, mothers, uncles, and aunts and cousins of the maidens and the young men went to that country of which the girl was Sultan, and the forty weddings were celebrated—may they all be blessed. Then the fathers and mothers and aunts and uncles and cousins returned alone to their homes, and since Shachbender had been of much service to them in getting their forty couples wedded, they sought, by way of thanks, to find a wife for him, too, and soon a most beautiful girl was found who was a match for him.

"But let us leave them and return to the girl who had become Sultan. Again there were brought to her some men who had broken her plaster portrait. They were the forty-one robbers who had attacked her and her companions on the island. She instantly recognized the evildoers and had them hanged.

"After all this was accomplished the girl who had become Sultan went up to the roof, to the arbor which had been allotted to her cousin, and asked him where he was from and how he came to that land. The youth wept and sobbed till his tears ran down to the floor, and told everything that had happened to him and the daughter of his uncle. Then the girl said, 'And if I now find your cousin for you, what shall you do then?' The young man flung himself down before the Sultan (as she seemed to be) and kissed her feet, crying, 'Then I will be your slave for ever and always.'

"Now when the youth's cousin, the Sultan, saw him at her feet, her love and passion, so long repressed, overwhelmed her. She bent to the floor and raised the youth and embraced and kissed him till the breath left her body. But the youth had no idea what was happening, and could not understand what the Sultan really wanted. Then she threw off all her royal robes, and cried, 'Then look!' At that, the eyes of the youth were opened and he recognized who stood before him. He became as one possessed, and with joy they kissed and embraced one another till they had had their fill. They sat in the arbor and the girl told him everything that had happened from the day when they parted until that very hour, and she closed with the story of the daughter of the Grand Vizier, saying, 'You lost but one, now you have found two!' But he said, 'If you agree, it is all right.'

"Soon they betook themselves to the council of state and told how matters stood. There was no end to the astonishment, but finally the councillors said unanimously, 'Do not be troubled. Since he is your cousin, he shall be Sultan and you can be Queen, and you shall rule the realm together.' So it came about that the girl married her cousin and they ruled the kingdom together. Afterwards he also married the daughter of the Grand Vizier, and they all had children and grandchildren and lived happily ever after."

Now when the merchant's wife saw that the story of the manly maiden was ended, she got up and wanted to set off with the old woman to the supposed wedding. But at this moment the merchant appeared, just returned from his journey. He fell on his wife's neck and kissed her with many tears. But when he noticed that she was painted and powdered, and was going out, he began to suspect something and threateningly asked the old woman what sort of invitation it was. She made many excuses until, from fear of the merchant's threats, she told them the whole story, how she was supposed to take the wife to the Sultan's son, but that the goldfinch, by means of his stories, had kept her at home. When the merchant took the goldfinch in his hand and stroked him, saying, "Now I know why the dealer exclaimed, 'Who does not buy this bird shall regret it.' But now explain to me why he said, 'Who buys it for a thousand dinars shall also repent of it.'" "That I will gladly do," replied the goldfinch, "only open your hand, and you will see at once." The merchant opened his hand and the goldfinch unfolded his wings, rose into the air, and disappeared.

The Sultan's son, we are told, died of love and the Sultan caused the old woman, who had so long put him off with lies, to be drowned.

That happened to them, but this happened to us. On their roof is sheep dung, on ours, almonds and raisins. If we have spoken the truth, it is God's truth; if we have lied, God forgive us. Go home quickly, or the dog will eat up your supper, and forgive us for wearying you. We in turn forgive you for being such a nuisance to us.

Cracker or
Because of the Calf and Something More

Once upon a time there were a man and his wife who had only one child and were exceedingly poor. The man died, leaving nothing but a calf. After his father died the son asked his mother what his name was, and she told him, "You don't have any name." Then he said, "Give me some money with which to buy one." She said, "We have no money, but if you care to take the calf, you are welcome to it." The son took the calf and went along till he met seven robbers. They asked him what he wanted, and when he had told them, they took away the calf, and said, "You are called Cracker." Full of delight he hastened back to his mother, and cried out, "Mother, now I have got a name." "Well, what is it?" asked the mother. "Oh, dear!" he said, "I have forgotten it." So he forthwith hurried back to the robbers and asked them about his name. They gave him a pitcher, and said, "When you get back to your mother smash the pitcher, and the pitcher will go 'crack' and you will remember your name." He did as he was told, but his mother was very angry, and said, "Alas! You have done away with our only possession and you have simply been made a fool of." He answered, "Now, Mother, you'll see, they will catch it because of the calf and something more."

As soon as his mother had given him some broken bracelets, he planted them in the soil of their garden and began to water the spot. The seven robbers came by and asked him what he was doing. He said, "This soil has the property, when wheat is sown in it, of bringing forth silver." "How is that?" they asked. Then he pulled a few pieces of the broken bracelets out of the ground and showed them to the robbers. As soon as they saw it, they bought the piece of ground at a high price. They sowed wheat, but the earth gave nothing but wheat. Then they denounced Cracker to the judge. But he brought witnesses that the robbers had seen for themselves how silver grew from the ground; they just didn't have the same luck that he had. The judge dismissed them, and Cracker consoled them by saying that he had an even better proposition for them. He took a donkey and stuck a nugget of gold into his backside; then when he prodded its behind with a stick, the donkey dropped the gold. As soon as the seven robbers saw that Cracker's donkey dropped gold, they bought it for a great sum of money. But Cracker said, "Take care, for this donkey eats only almonds and raisins and passes gold but once a week. For this he must be taken into the best room in the upper story where fine rugs have to be spread and many porcelain cups put, and many lamps have to be lit there and mirrors put all about the room." The robbers did exactly as Cracker had explained and they waited all night long expectantly at the door of the room. Now as soon as the donkey saw the many lamps gleaming in the mirrors and his own reflection coming at him from all sides, he went mad and raged around the room until all the lamps, mirrors, and porcelain cups were broken and the rugs were torn to shreds. But when they heard the noise the robbers were highly delighted; they thought, What a lot of gold the donkey has produced, only listen how it chinks and clatters! But when, in the morning, they went into the room and saw what the donkey had done, they ran straightway to the judge to denounce Cracker. But he brought witnesses that the donkey had produced gold in front of the robbers' eyes. If the robbers had not succeeded, they just hadn't had the same luck as he had had. The judge realized that Cracker was right and dismissed the robbers.

When they saw that they could not get hold of Cracker by lawful means, they seized him and stuffed him into a sack, intending to drown him in a pond. On the way they came to an inn, and, going in to refresh themselves, they left Cracker lying outside. Cracker shouted for help. By chance, a herdsman whom he knew passed by with his flock, and asked him, "What is the matter?" Then Cracker cried, "Woe is me! They want to marry me to the daughter of the Sultan and have put me into this accursed sack to take me to her." The herdsman said, "Do you want to exchange with me?" "With pleasure," said Cracker. The herdsman undid the sack and let Cracker out, then crept into it himself. Cracker tied it up, took the flock, and made off. But the robbers picked up the sack with the herdsman in it and threw it into the pond.

Next day the robbers again passed by this pond and great was their astonishment at suddenly seeing Cracker, with a huge flock, standing before them. "How did you get here?" they called out. "Is it the Day of Resurrection already?" "Far from it," replied Cracker, "but don't you know that at the bottom of the pond the most beautiful treasures can be got?" He led them down to the edge of the pond, where the reflection of the beasts of his herd could be seen, and shouted out, "Just look down there! I got the whole of this herd of sheep and oxen from down there, so now I have all that I want, thank you!" Then the robbers' mouths watered, and they said to Cracker, "Perhaps you will be good enough to throw us into the pond so that we may get a fine herd like that, too?" Cracker was ready and willing and he wanted to set to work at once, but they suggested, "Had we better perhaps wait till evening for this?" "On no account," replied Cracker, "the water herds hide during the night, and then you will get nothing." "Well, if there's no other way . . ." said the robbers, and let themselves be thrown into the water one by one. After this had been accomplished Cracker went to the robbers' house, took everything that was in it, and carried it all to his mother, saying, "Look, Mother, this was because of the calf and something more."

From now on they were rich, and lived happily to the end of their days. On their roof is sheep dung, but on ours are almonds and raisins.

A Love Song

While the men sing only on certain occasions, such as the Sabbath, at festivals, and at circumcisions and wedding ceremonies, and then only religious songs (which, however, are often allegorical and erotic in character), the women accompany their work, such as milling and the other activities of their daily life, with songs of purely worldly content. These songs are rather varied in form and theme, and the following, which comes from a very young girl, has, except for the last part, which is in rhyme, no other form than a certain inner rhythm, recognizable in the translation.

The Goat Girl and Her Suitor

"Go a step further, man, let the flocks graze.
Are you thirsty? Then drink; you have two hands
  and there is the trough.
But if you want milk, there my goats are, already
  with kid."
"I want neither your milk nor your water, it is you
  I want, goat girl."

"Away with your hand from my hand, you are break-
  ing my bracelet,
This armlet is gold, there is no other smith like the
  one who made it."
"Cursed be the father of the bracelet, another will
  be bought for you from the market."
"Away with your hand from my hand. By God,
  don't curse my father."

"I'm not cursing your father: your father is my uncle." [1]

"Away with your hand from my hand. By God, don't curse my brother."

"I'm not cursing your brother: your brother is my brother-in-law."

"Away with your hand from my hand. By God, don't curse my mother."

"I'm not cursing your mother: your mother is my aunt." [2]

"Oh, would I were a blossom of basil that I might be an ornament in my father's hair!" [3]

"Yes, you be the blossom; but I shall pluck you."

"Oh, would I were a turban wound round my father's head!"

"Yes, you be the turban; but I shall put you on."

"Oh, would I were a stone walled in my father's house!"

"Yes, you be the stone; but I shall break you off."

"Oh, would I were a tree planted in my father's yard!"

"Yes, you be the tree; but I shall fell you."

"Oh, would I were a snake wound round my father's head!"

"Yes, you be the snake; but I shall kill you."

"Sun, sun, don't set, my goats are still hungry.

[1] That is, father-in-law.
[2] That is, mother-in-law.
[3] Where none would dare take it away.

My burden is up on the mountain and my bobbin is
   not yet full." [1]
"Mother, tell my father, I don't want to be a goat
   girl any longer;
The girls have all married, only I still tend the flock.
The pasture on the mountains has disappeared,
And the troughs are all dry."

"O you who go up the mountains, come down the
   slopes,
I charge you with seventy oaths, bound on camels,
   that they be heavily burdened thereby,
That thus you speak to the chief of the village:

'The crop sprouts, and comes up,
Let him come to pluck it—
But if he come not, it is doomed to die.' "

---

[1] The goat girl spins while she is out with her flock during the day.
She must besides collect wood, which she carries home on her head in
the evening.

Yemenite Aggadot

The education of the average Yemenite is derived exclusively from Jewish sources and in general is the same as that of the Orthodox Jews of Eastern Europe. Only two points should be noticed as distinctive: the Yemenite, from childhood on, gets a very precise knowledge of the text of the Bible, and even an ordinary man can recite a considerable part of it by heart. From this, as from the daily study of the Mishna, they get their excellent knowledge of Hebrew. The Babylonian Talmud, on the other hand, is only studied by scholars, while the simple folk are nourished abundantly by the Aggadot in its most various forms. This tendency in the selection of educational material, probably a very ancient one, is to be attributed to the strong inwardness that disinguishes the religious life of the Yemenites, and it is surely no accident that there have been preserved only among the Yemenites a number of precious old Midrashim and devotional books. The following Aggadot are taken from those which evidently were written in Yemen itself.

Worth Teaching

Someone came to Rabbi Akiva and asked him to instruct him in the secret teaching about the creation of the world. Rabbi Akiva asked him, "Are you hungry or satisfied?" He said, "I am neither satisfied nor hungry; he who is satisfied, and does not say grace, trespasses; he who is hungry, and does not eat, sins." Then Rabbi Akiva said, "Come, I will teach you, for you are worthy of it."

A woman came to Rabbi Akiva, and asked, "Why were the children of Israel not condemned to death when they committed the great sin of worshipping the Golden Calf?" The master looked at her, and said, "What do you want here? For the whole wisdom of a woman is only in spinning, as it is written: 'And all the women that were wise-hearted did spin with their hands.' " He gave his pupils a sign and they drove her out. But then the pupils said, "You put her off with a blade of straw; but what can you say to us about it?" Rabbi Akiva said, "Only the fools worshipped the Golden Calf. The people of understanding did not worship it."

God's Business

When our wise men were journeying in upper Galilee they met a wolf prowling in front of the door of a deserted synagogue; when they saw this they wept. At that the wolf opened his mouth and said, "Why do you weep?" They said, "For the house of God, which lies desolate." The wolf said, "One day this synagogue will be full of the pupils of wise men, on the day when God will set up Zion. But go your ways."

They did so, but soon met another wolf who asked them, "Where are you going?" They said, "About our business." The wolf said, "You poor creatures! One day it will be held against you that you were pursuing your own affairs and did not

concern yourselves with God's business." They said,
"And where do you come from? What business of
God's do you look after?" "I come from out of my
den, and now am on the way to do a good deed. A
bridegroom has sinned today, and I must go along
and eat him up."

The Curse

When our father Jacob was blessing Reuben, Simeon,
and Levi, he said, "Cursed be their anger, for it
was fierce." The earth trembled and the attendant
angels cried out, "From this time ill shall befall
the tribes of Israel for in truth this is no blessing."
Then a voice came from heaven, which cried,
"Reuben is not therewith accursed, but the Power of
Evil." Then the Power of Evil said, "I was created
first, before the Power of Good; I am the firstborn;
if Reuben is forgiven because of the right of the
firstborn, I, who have not sinned, must surely be
pardoned." And Jacob continued, "And their wrath,
for it was cruel." Then the Power of Evil was glad,
and said to himself, "Yes, certainly the wrath was
cursed, and not I."

Zion and the Torah

"A redeemer will come to Zion, and unto them that
turn from transgression in Jacob." Should not
Jacob, that is to say, Israel, have been named before
Zion? The answer is thus: "So long as Zion remains

unharmed the Torah remains unharmed; but so long as Zion is not rebuilt, the Torah will be ever less in Israel."

The Inner Light

The light that has been created becomes neither more nor less; but the inner light grows without ceasing, as it is said: "A great voice that ceases not."

Legends of the Learned

Legends about the great deeds, mainly miraculous (*peullot*), of the scholars, even of those who are alive or recently deceased, are some of the favorite material for stories among the men. Those of the second type given here are more frequent than those of the first.

How Maimuni Conquered His Adversary
or Imagination Kills

A favorite Arabic catchword runs: "Today you are going to get something to drink, you *Kammun*!" However, the *Kammun* (Arabic for the caraway plant) is never watered; the meaning, therefore, is: You will never get anything. The following story is a Midrash based upon this catchword, a form of story which is very popular with the Yemenites.

Rabbi Moshe ben Maimon, apart from his splendid gifts as teacher of the Law and master of philosophy, was also an outstanding doctor. His reputation in this science was so great that the Sultan of Egypt made him his personal physician. Many doctors begrudged him this high position, and with all their might sought to remove him from his exalted place. One doctor among them, named Kammun, which means "caraway," had the best prospect, having many influential friends at court. These were soon aware that the Sultan was dependent on Rabbi Moshe and placed unbounded confidence in him. They suggested that he should take Kammun as a second personal physician, in order that the care of the royal health might not be left to the wisdom of a single man and especially not to a Jew. "Two personal physicians are no use," asserted the Sultan, "but since you tell me so much about Kammun I will put both of them to the test, and whoever proves himself the greater master of his profession shall be my personal physician." Soon afterwards, the Sultan summoned the two of them and when they had come before him, he said, turning to Kammun as he did so: "They have told me that you are an even greater physician than Maimuni; but I do not want to rely on the statements of others, but to make trial of your ability for myself. I will set you a task whose accomplishment will give me a clear proof of the superiority of the victor. You shall each try to poison the other, and whoever succeeds in remaining alive through wisely chosen antidotes shall be my personal physician."

When Kammun heard these words he was delighted, because he was in fact a notorious poisoner, and many highly placed persons had been put out of the way through his medicines without the cause ever becoming known. But Rabbi Moshe ben Maimon was deeply grieved, for he was now in the terrible position of either committing murder or being killed. Soon Kammun, experienced in such matters, had found means to get poison mixed with the food which Rabbi Moshe ate. But Rabbi Moshe knew how to render each poison harmless by an antidote; and everyone was astonished each day when he appeared at court to find him still alive and in blooming health. But what did Rabbi Moshe do in order to free himself from Kammun? Nothing whatsoever. He would not have the blood of another on his hands, in spite of the sage who had said: If any man goes about to kill you, forestall him by killing him.

Only, when he saw Kammun, as he daily did at court, he said to him in passing, "Today you will get the poison to drink, Kammun; today you are going to get something to drink!" Kammun carefully analyzed all the food and drink that he took, but could discover no trace of poison in them. The people at court constantly asked him, "What has Maimuni given you today?" He was ashamed to show his ignorance, and said each time, "He put this and that in my food, and I have taken this and that as antidote." Now, as he could not discover the nature of the poison in question, he feared that it was a creeping, slow-working substance, and soon refrained from eating any food at all. The only thing he took was some milk, from a cow that was milked before his eyes. He became paler and weaker day by day, while Maimuni, with his health intact, went about his business.

One day, while holding a half-empty jar of milk in his hand, he encountered Maimuni in one of the anterooms of the Sultan's palace. Maimuni immediately said to him, "Now you are drinking it, Kammun!" This frightened him to death, for he could think nothing else than that he had taken the deadly poison. He scarcely had the strength to place the jar on the table; then he fell to the ground and passed away.

The news of it spread like wind through the town, and soon all the doctors and alchemists gathered together to investigate the drink with which Maimuni had done the renowned poisoner to death. But Maimuni had a suckling child brought in and, in front of all, gave it the rest of the milk, and behold, nothing in the slightest happened to the child! There was no end to their astonishment, and everyone was convinced that Maimuni had overcome his enemy by sorcery. But Maimuni answered, "There is no sorcery in Jacob, and no black art in Israel, but there is a little proverb that even the galley slave on the ship knows, and with this counsel I mastered my adversary." Thereupon he told them the whole story, and so all came to know that Kammun died of nothing but unfounded fears, as the proverb says: "Imagination kills." The Sultan was greatly pleased at the wisdom of his personal physician and rewarded him royally, saying, "Now I know that you are truly a great doctor, because you heal not only the body but the soul as well."

Yih'ya Tabib

Yih'ya Tabib, or Zechariah Harofe, as he is called in Hebrew, the author of the Midrash *Hahefetz*, was fabulously learned. After he had mastered all that was to be learned in Yemen, he traveled, with great privation and suffering, to the most distant part of

India, where seven doctors lived who knew more medicine than any doctor in the world. But they were at great pains to disclose nothing of their art to anyone. So Yih'ya employed a ruse. He knocked at the door of their house, and when they opened it to him, he made it clear to them by signs that he was deaf and dumb and wished to be their servant. They accepted him gladly, taking him for a deaf-mute, and thus he stayed with them for twelve years. He examined each sick person who came to the seven doctors, in advance, so that he knew what was the matter with him, and then, when they prescribed the remedy, he came to know the wonderful methods which these Indian doctors used.

One day a seriously ill man was brought in. Yih'ya examined him and found that only one artery was still working. When the seven doctors saw the sick man, his case appeared to them to be hopeless, and they wanted to give him a powder to spare him the torments of death. Yih'ya, however, sprang from his place and cried out, "What are you doing? Don't you see that there is still one artery working in him?" and showed them the place. The doctors were not a little astonished, first, that the supposed deaf-mute could speak, and further, that he knew more about medicine than they did. They prescribed the necessary remedy for the sick man and allowed him to be taken home. Then they said to Yih'ya, "Truly, you deserve death, for you have mocked our beards and stolen our learning. But first tell us about yourself."

Yih'ya said, "I am from Yemen, and in our land many sick people who might be cured die because nobody knows the right treatments. Now, if it is your wish, I will never again treat a sick person and will let them all die, but the responsibility shall fall on you." Because the doctors saw that his intentions were good, they said to him, "As we have taught you till now against our will, from now on we will teach you of our own free will. For really you do not know anything as yet; when you have passed the examination which we shall set you, we shall give you a certificate." Each of the seven doctors had, as it happened, some disability—one was lame, another deaf, and so on. Yih'ya succeeded in curing them all, so they gave him the right to practice, and he returned to Yemen, where he became personal physician to the Imam.

One day, the son of the Imam was found murdered in the forecourt of the synagogue. It was the act of men who were the enemies both of the Imam and the Jews. The Imam had all the Jews imprisoned and said to Yih'ya Tabib, "If you don't deliver up the murderer within three days, all the Jews shall be burnt. For since the body of my son was found in your synagogue, it is clear that one of you killed him." Yih'ya had the corpse taken and washed in warm water, then he took a quill pen which had written only the Torah, and wrote on the forehead of the dead man the first, middle, and last letters of the alphabet: *E Me T*, which signifies: Truth. Immediately the dead man began to speak and pointed out

the real murderers by name. The Imam embraced
his son and thanked Yih'ya for recalling him to life.
But Yih'ya said, "To do that, I have no permission,"
and wiped away the first of the three letters, leaving
Me T, which signifies: "Dead," and the youth was
again dead and speechless as before. The Imam took
vengeance on his enemies, the murderers, but let the
Jews go free, and from that time on nobody was
ever allowed to raise an accusation before him without proof.

A Prayer for Rain

It was said of Ibrahim, brother of Yih'ya Salih, who
was author of the *Etz Hayim* (regarded in Yemen as
canonical), that he wanted to impose his will upon
all, and even upon God. Once, when there was a
drought in the country, the whole community, as
they were wont to do in such cases, took the Torah
scrolls to the cemetery to pray for rain. Their
prayers were not heard, however, and they returned
to the town in shame. As they were taking the scrolls
of the Torah back into the synagogue, Ibrahim
stopped them, took up his stand in the forecourt of
the synagogue, and opening the Torah at a desk
which was brought there, cried out, "I will not stir
from this place until rain comes." He had scarcely
spoken when a severe hailstorm descended. Everyone
fell to the ground, giving thanks to God for the
wondrous answer; but the first hailstone, falling
from heaven, struck out Ibrahim's right eye, and
he wasted away because of it and died.

THE PAST

The Beginnings

In view of the ancient trade relations that existed between Palestine and southern Arabia, it would be in no way surprising if one were to come upon Jewish settlements in Yemen already in biblical times. Clear indications of a Jewish community in Yemen, and, incidentally, one in contact with Palestine, are first apparent in the fifth and sixth centuries of the Common Era, when the royal house of Yemen adopted Judaism. The following tales show how the Yemenites represent the beginnings of their own history.

How They Came to Yemen and Founded a Kingdom There

Our fathers came to Yemen forty-two years before the destruction of the First Temple. The prophet Jeremiah had repeatedly told them, "He that goeth forth from this city shall save his soul and live." And so seventy-five thousand God-fearing folk who took the word of the prophet to heart left the city. In the van were twenty-five of the noblest families, whose names are still remembered; they crossed the Jordan and turned towards the desert, traversing once again the paths over which the children of Israel had come to the country in Moses' time. Speaking of their emigration the prophet Jeremiah says, "Judah is gone into a peaceful exile," meaning: not driven out by enemies did those men leave Jerusalem, but following the word of God. From Edom the emigrants turned south, until they reached

Yemen and the valley of Sanaa. In his kindly prescience the Holy One, praised be He, had transferred a strip of the Holy Land to that place, as was witnessed by the fact that all the plants necessary for fulfilment of the religious duties grow in this country; for instance, the four species of the lulav.

Among the emigrants were all classes of the people of Judah: priests, Levites, Israelites, slaves, and proselytes. Even today the Jews in Sanaa say of the hamlets in the different districts of Yemen that they are descended from proselytes and slaves, and that is why they are so backward in knowledge of the Torah, in cleanliness, and in the decencies of life; and that is also why they do not intermarry with them.

The Levites settled mostly in particular towns, as they had been accustomed to do in Eretz Israel, and there are to this day in Yemen localities inhabited only by Levites. So strong was their feeling that they were still in the Holy Land that they designated certain Levite cities as places of refuge for those who had committed manslaughter; and today there may still be read upon the rock near such a place the words, *miklat, miklat,* which is to say, "Here the road leads to the place of refuge." This is the more remarkable since the practice was first established in Palestine when the kingdom of Israel lay on both sides of the Jordan; Moses did not use such places because in his time the entire country was not wholly under Israel's rule.

All the noble families had pedigrees, and thus

everyone preserved the tradition of his origin in the Holy Land, until some two hundred and fifty years ago. At that time it happened that Mori Aharon Iraki, who came to Yemen from Egypt, and who, for his piety, wealth, and high standing with the court, had gained a great reputation among his fellow believers, desired a wife for his son from among the noble families of Sanaa. But all whom he approached demanded that by producing his genealogy he should prove that he, like they, stood in the unbroken line of succession from one of the noble generations of Judah. So he employed a ruse. He asked for their pedigrees, and when he got them all together, burned them, saying, "All Jews are noble, there must be no distinctions made among them." The Salikh family alone preserved its genealogy, and only two of the priestly families still know from which of the twenty-four Temple guards they are descended.

Now, after the Jews had settled in Yemen they rapidly became rulers of the country; in fact, they were habitual warriors, and having departed in peace from Jerusalem and not in hasty flight, they were able to bring all their weapons and their wealth with them. When they had become rulers of the valley of Sanaa, which was so like Palestine, they held it almost as holy as if it were Eretz Israel itself.

How They Did Not Obey Ezra's Call
to Return to Jerusalem

When God took pity on his people through Cyrus and Ezra, and Ezra sent a message to all who were scattered abroad that they should go up with him to Zion, chosen of God, only the poor and mean obeyed his call; the noble-born remained in Babylon. The message also reached the Jews in Yemen, but they would not listen to it, for they realized in their innermost mind that the Second Temple would also be destroyed; so they did as the nobles in Babylon, fulfilling in themselves the words of the Song of Songs: "I have put off my coat; how shall I put it on?" They did ill by opposing the prophet Ezra and not returning to Zion. If they and those in Babylon had all of them gone up to Jerusalem, Israel's merit before God would have been great, and the majesty of God would have chosen Zion as an enduring dwelling place; and there would have come no second destruction of the Temple.

The Jews of Yemen, because of this sin, were punished with poverty and misery, and the prophet and sage laid his curse of exile on them, saying, "Whosoever came not within three days, all his substance should be forfeited, and himself separated from the congregation." For this reason no property was left to the people of Yemen and no great estate survived. May the Holy One, praised be He, have pity on their poverty and wretchedness.

How It Came About That Their Power
Was Broken

At that time the dwellers in the land were pagans,
poor in understanding and in state. They could not
thrive in the face of the wisdom and wealth of the
Jews. All of the community were punctiliously exact
in their dealings with the pagans as regards mine and
thine, as it is said: "The remnant of Israel shall not
do iniquity, nor speak lies, neither shall a deceitful
tongue be found in their mouth."

Once it so happened that a pagan was driven out
of Palestine to Yemen. There the heathen asked him
what they should do to gain mastery over the Jews.
Sly as Balaam, he replied thus: "The God of these
people loves justice and hates robbery; tempt them
so that they turn aside from their straight path, then
their God will abandon them."

At that time Jewish skill in the silversmith's art
was famous and unequaled. So the pagan went to a
silversmith, bringing him some bars of silver, and
asked him to make a pendant out of them. Before his
eyes the silversmith weighed up the bars and set to
work. When the pagan came back to collect the
pendant, the silversmith wanted to weigh the ornament in order to show the customer that not an ounce
had been lost. But he said, "Who will doubt the honor
of a Jew?" Subsequently all the pagans did as he
had done; they never allowed the ornaments to be
weighed, and asked no questions about the unused
silver.

There were found, for our sins, a few wretched creatures who fell into this trap, and misused the trust placed in them. Thus the power of the Jews declined, as it is said: "One sinner destroyeth much good," and from now on the heathen began to master them.

Mohammed's Letter of Protection

Islamic religious law, which is based on the Koran and on sayings attributed to Mohammed, is the law of the realm in Yemen, and thus it also defines the legal position of the Jews. It is not surprising, therefore, that the Jews have expressed their desire for the safeguarding or betterment of their position in the form of a letter of protection ascribed to Mohammed. This letter—written, naturally, in Hebrew characters—was widely known among the Yemenites, and is ultimately traced back to an actual document of Mohammed's which already in the early Middle Ages had been completely altered. In its present form it reflects Yemenite social conditions.

This is the letter of protection which the prophet Mohammed, may peace and mercy and God's blessing be with him, caused to be written for the children of Israel.

When the heathen were pressing hard against the prophet, may peace be with him, the children of Israel came to him, saying, "We are with you and on your side; we will fight against the unbelievers until you have peace with them." And thus they did, fighting all the week until at noon on Friday the prophet said to them, "Children of Israel, go and keep your Sabbath. With God's help we will fight off the enemy alone, though it be hard." But the children of Israel answered, "Prophet of God, dearer to us than life or possessions, for us there is no Sabbath whilst you have no peace." So they joined battle again. The sun went down and the children of Israel desecrated the Sabbath, fighting on until they had conquered the heathen. When the prophet heard of this his joy was great, and he said, "Men of Israel, by God's grace I will reward you for your goodness and for all time give you my protection and my vow, until the Day of Resurrection."

To his companions, the prophet said, "Allah has bidden me wed Safiya, a maiden of the children of Israel; what say you?" "Prophet of Allah," replied his companions, "what you do is well done; prophecy and true wisdom are yours." So it was that the prophet married Safiya.

Then he called all his companions together and the elders and scribes as well as Abdullah ibn Salam, the Jewish sage, and in their presence ordered his son-in-law, Ali, to write the letter of protection. Ali took some paper and a quill and wrote the following exactly as the prophet dictated it to him:

"In the name of God, the merciful, the all-compassionate. Listen and hear, all Muslims and believers, both absent and present. Let the children of Israel return to their villages and their strongholds, and dwell in them, they and all their generations to come. God, praised be He, and the Muslims and believers warrant for their safety, for as comrades under my protection, I accepted them and I am answerable for them. Let no insults, abuse, accusations, and hostile acts take place in any town, village, or market place of Muslims and true believers. Illegal levies, fines, and special taxes of any kind may not be demanded of them; their fields and vineyards and palm groves are free of tithe; they have only to pay the head tax, and the rich who ride on horseback must pay three pieces of silver a year.[1] The poor who have only food for a month and clothing for a year are to pay what they can afford. A man of trust from among them is to collect the head tax.

"Whoever takes anything from the children of Israel unjustly, though it is no greater in weight than an ant, shall not have the blessing of God, and I will testify against him on the Day of Resurrection. The protected comrades are not forbidden to enter the mosques, the tombs of the saints, and the Koran schools.[2] They are not to be prevented from riding on horseback. They are to wear a girdle by which they may be recognized as protected comrades, and none shall harm them.

"They must not change their religion for any other; they must not desecrate the Sabbath by any kind of work; they must not be disturbed in reading the Torah which was revealed through Moses, peace be with him, who spoke with God on Mount Sinai; neither must they be disturbed at their prayers in the synagogues, nor when they are attending the schools and baths, nor when preparing intoxicating liquor for their own use.

"This is their reward because they, the children of

[1] The Jews in Yemen, however, are forbidden to ride on horseback, and in some regions are not even allowed to ride on donkeys.
[2] The Koran schools in small towns serve as lodging houses and in a few less fanatical districts they are open to the Jews, who, as itinerant craftsmen, often spend a week at a time in purely Arab localities.

Israel, fought for me and desecrated the Sabbath on my account. I call Allah to witness, O Muslims and true believers, that you may watch over and preserve my letter of protection and seal.

"Given on the twentieth day of Ramadan in the year nine. Such and such were witnesses. Ali wrote it."

The Exile to Mauza and Mori Salim Shebezi

At the time when European Jewry was shaken on the one hand by the Sabbatai Zevi movement, and on the other by the Chmielnicki rebellion and other persecutions, the Yemenite Jews also had their special hour. There lived at that time Mori Salim Shebezi, greatest of their holy men, who left, in addition to a famous Kabbalistic work,[1] innumerable religious poems which are said to be still sung to the tunes which the author gave them. And that was the time when the exile to Mauza took place, in many ways the most decisive event in their later history.

The Exile to Mauza

The Jews of Sanaa at the present time live in a city of their own surrounded by a separate wall; but it was not always so. In earlier times, on the contrary, the site was within Sanaa itself, and even today mosques which once were synagogues bear names indicating the site of the former Jewish quarter. The change took place in those hard times when the Arabs drove the Turks out of Yemen by decade-long wars and when hunger, pestilence, and famine ruined the land.

At that time there ruled a tyrannical Imam who first permitted the places of worship of the Jews to be destroyed and then concluded an agreement with his neighbors, who were small princes, to drive the Jews out of the Yemen hill country. This was occa-

[1] The traditional view that the Kabbalistic work *Hemdat Yamim* was written by Shebezi, is now contested by competent scholars.

sioned, it is said, by the love of a princess of the house of Imam for a Jew, and the child she had by him. In the year 1988,[2] shortly before the Passover feast at a time when men hope for salvation, the famous and wealthy community of Sanaa and many other great communities went into exile. Because of the difficulty of the road, they could take but a few of their precious books with them; the greater part they gave for safekeeping to an Arab friend. But the Arab betrayed the trust placed in him and burned the books, and the few they had with them were for the most part lost in the confusion of their exile. That is why so little of the old writings has remained. The Mauza region to which they were banished is hot and fever-ridden, and because they were accustomed to mountain air, and in addition were suffering from hunger and the strain of traveling, most of them perished.

At that time there lived in Ta'izz, outside the limits fixed by the decree, Mori Salim Shebezi. He bewailed the plight of the exiles in many songs, and at last—perhaps through his influence with the ruler of the country, or, as others say, because the Imam and his house were afflicted with great suffering by a miracle of Shebezi's—he made the Imam and the other princes recall the Jews. Certainly they did not allow them to return to their old dwelling places; outside the walls of Sanaa a place was set apart for them, where they built a city of their own which, because of their industry and aptitude, soon became a great and flourishing settlement.

[2] According to the Seleucid reckoning. It corresponds to 1677.

120

Mori Salim Shebezi—His Own Testimony

As our fathers tell, there appeared in the year 5379 [1619] two comets in the east with tails looking like sticks; one was visible for fifteen days and the other for forty, and people believed that they were the stars which announce the coming of the Messiah. I found that the scribe Israel ben Joseph Mashta has recorded that I, Shalom ben Joseph Mashta, who am the meanest of all scholars, was born in that year, and named Shebezi after the place of my birth. And now the year 5406 [1646] has come, and we still await the Messiah.

The Holy Man in Life and after His Death

Mori Salim was an ascetic and a holy man and most learned in all knowledge. His contemporaries believed that the great suffering which in those days was the lot of the Yemenite Jews, from hunger, pestilence, and persecution, portended time's ending, and that none other than Mori Salim was the Messiah. In the messianic year 5408 [1648] he was exactly thirty years of age, and that would be just the age when the Messiah, like Joseph, would begin his ministry. But they still waited as the years went on, thinking that perhaps, like Moses, he would obey his call at eighty years of age. But Mori Salim opposed those who expressed such ideas and called them idiots. And even if liberation did not come through him, he healed the nation's heart with his songs, for they express the bonds of love between God and Israel, the

121

sufferings of the Galut, and the yearning for Zion in words ever new and precious, and their meaning is often evident only to the initiated. Even if it was not permitted to him to dwell in Eretz Israel, it is known that he often went to Jerusalem, or to the holy city of Safed, on the eve of the Sabbath, and spent the Sabbath there. Even after his death he never ceased to be a source of salvation.

From all parts of Yemen annual pilgrimages were made to his tomb in Ta'izz and many things have been reported of the wonderful cures which the spring near his grave brought about, both for Jews and for non-Jews. But just as in life Mori Salim desired no honors, so he scorned them in death; and as often as they would whitewash his grave or set a dome over it, the lime would flake off and the building disintegrate, until some two generations ago a Turkish officer, whose wife was miraculously cured through the holy man's blessing, caused a tomb to be built. He bade the spirit of the holy man receive it as a thank offering in honor of God, and not as his own. The building has remained and the whitewash has not flaked from the gravestone.

Mori Yih'ya al-Abyad—How He Wrote the Torah

Mori Yih'ya was a pious man without blemish from the town of Sanaa. There are to this day in the synagogues of Sanaa Torah scrolls written by his holy hand. He used to write the Torah thus: He took parchment, quill, and ink, and clambered into a fiery glowing furnace and there he wrote the divine name of God; then he clambered out and completed the remaining words on either side of the name of God. The Torah scrolls written by him had a wonderful property; immediately when anyone who was impure in his body or his mind went to read from them on the Sabbath, the parchment turned yellow and the letters faded. Because of this his Torah scrolls are held most holy, and today are no longer used for reading.

Washing the Dead

This famous Mori died in the desert. It was at the time of the exile to Mauza. A party of the exiles wanted to go to Eretz Israel, but not knowing the way they got lost in the desert. They wandered for many days without finding water; when a sandstorm overtook them, the aged Mori could no longer stand, but sinking to the ground he passed away. They did not know what to do about burying him as they had no water for washing the corpse. Then a miracle happened to them through the goodness of the holy man. A spring of water rose in the place where they were to wash the corpse. Whoever wanted to drink and wished to replenish his water bottle might do so. Directly Mori Yih'ya had been washed and buried, the spring dried up and the ground was as though it had never been there. Soon, too, the Sultan Safi-ed-Din came with a great host and much provisions and led them in honor back to their native Sanaa.

From an Old Chronicle

A Dream

Even today dreams and portents count for much. The following dream came to the chronicler during the time of famine and apostasy described in the section which follows.

In the month of Sivan of that year I had the following dream: I was going as usual into the synagogue of Mori Haiyim Hallevi, blessed be his memory, and as I came into the courtyard of the synagogue and was about to go into the house, I saw the whole holy congregation turned towards the south, its back to the Ark of the Torah and Jerusalem, softly praying. I cried aloud and fell on my face, saying: O God, despoil us not because of these. As I rose I saw Mori Mose-al-Gatii, who alone was not praying with the congregation but studied the Talmud in a corner. I went up to him, saying: Mori, why don't you stop these people who reverse our ordinances, made from the beginning of the world, and pray towards the south. The Mori answered: My son, I have begged every one of them to leave off their folly, but none has obeyed me. As soon as I heard these words I fell again to the ground and cried: O God, wilt thou ruin the rest of thy people because of these? Whilst I lay thus, there appeared an angel in the air who resembled those depicted in the books of the Torah, and hovered slowly round, flying low like a vulture. Then he walked through the gate of the courtyard, and saw through the window the congregation praying towards the south. He looked two or three times through the door of the synagogue as though to make sure that he had seen aright. I rose to my feet and went up to him and bade him offer intercession for Israel. But he answered nothing and taking a stick in his hand as though to say, Now wait, you will soon see what the end will be, he disappeared. Blessed be the All knowing.

Hunger

Famines are of frequent occurrence in Yemen, where, as a result of centuries of mismanagement, the rich irrigation resources are inadequately used. On this account the Jews, who usually had no land and were entirely dependent on purchasing their provisions, suffered most.

Now came famine. Famine destroying all wealth, famine making men pull down their houses to sell the timber for a crust of bread, famine scattering the congregations to the four winds, famine making men neglect the Torah and their prayers so that many synagogues were closed on workdays, and on the Sabbath and feast days stood empty, famine driving the children from the schools into the markets and into the non-Jewish streets to scrape up something. Many ate straw and matting, others collected worms from the dung heap, swallowing them down. The most loathsome diseases spread and many people went mad from starvation. And if the non-Jews were badly off, how much worse off were the Jews! It went so far at last that from grief and weakness men neglected their merciful duty to bury the dead. When a man had died nobody came to bury him. If there was one prepared to do it, he did not carry the dead man to the grave in festive clothing as was right, but in rags; only two or three people went with him to the graveyard, and there was no procession or funeral rite; no Kaddish was said and even the gravedigger lightened his work by simply laying the dead man in the earth instead of digging a proper grave. And for our sins, the mourners sat with none to console them, alone and deserted. As it is said, "I have taken away My peace from this people, and mercy and compassion." Mercy, that is to say, the burial of the dead; and compassion, that is, comfort to the mourners.

[*A year later.*] The famine has now become worse; seven hundred and fifty souls, mostly women, have forsaken their faith; the Imam gives relief, food and drink, only to converts.

[*Two months later.*] Let us fall on the earth and with hands and feet outstretched thank God that He has not utterly destroyed us. On the fifteenth of Av, God blessed the earth with rain, which fell day and night until the twentieth of Elul. Let us sing His praises in a song of thankfulness for each and every drop.

Shalom Shar'abi

The Tabernacle

Mori Shalom was of the people of Shar'ab, distin-
guished for their great learning and piety. For the
most part they were weavers by trade, having chosen
this somewhat mechanical craft because it left the
thoughts and tongue free for studying the Torah;
when they sat together at work it seemed as though
the words of the Torah flew to and fro with the shut-
tle. And when they went to the weekly market to sell
their cloth, they spoke by the way only of holy things.
Once, as they were going to market, they were speaking of the building of the tabernacle, and they could
not agree about certain details so they took all their
beautifully worked cloths from the asses and began
to model the tabernacle according to the size and
colors, and before they knew it the tabernacle stood
in front of them exactly as it was built by Moses at
God's instruction. But they were not permitted to
admire their handiwork for long, for a fire came
down from heaven and snatched them and the tabernacle away. The place where this happened is still
known; it was fenced round when they found that
the impure who enter there come to harm.

Flight to Jerusalem

Once Shalom Shar'abi went to the city of the Muslims to sell his cloth. There the wife of a great one

saw him from her window and fell in love with him, for his face was made beautiful with the light of the Torah. She had him brought up to her upper room, there to show his cloths, but directly they were alone she shut the door and declared her desire. Mori Shalom acted as though he were ready to do her will, proposing that they should go up to the roof together where they could be alone to their hearts' delight. This he did because the windows were too narrow to allow a man to pass through them; and so, as soon as they had reached the roof, having first made a great vow in case he should remain alive, he threw himself down into the courtyard. Although the roof was five stories high he escaped unharmed, and made his way on foot towards Jerusalem. On arrival there he sat down modestly in a corner of the Bet-El synagogue, but was soon recognized as the great holy man he was, and his name lives to this day in Jerusalem as the founder of the brotherhood which in this synagogue carries on, in Kabbalistic fashion, their ecstatic practice of prayer.

The Last Messiah

Several times Messiahs have appeared in Yemen. This fact is largely explained by the "superstition" of the Jews there. Yet it must be remembered that the Imam, ruler of central Yemen, is regarded as divinely inspired, and that every usurper in the country—and when has there not been one?— must show spiritual qualities in order to achieve the dignity of Imam. So it is not surprising that not only the Messiah of the twelfth century, famous because of the missive of Maimonides, but also the Messiah of the nineteenth century, spoken of in the following letters, found followers among the Arabs. It was even proposed to the latter Messiah that he embrace Islam and announce himself as Calif. And it is Islamic and not Jewish religious law if he, as a sign of his messianic rulership, levied tithe from the Jews. In 1893 details about a Messiah were still being reported, but his sphere of activity was limited in extent. (His son is living today, in Tel-Aviv.) The last Jewish "Messiah" actually to start a kind of movement appeared in Yemen in the sixties of the last century. There were actually two: the first was "genuine," a true preacher of repentance and an ascetic who paid for his pretensions with death; the second, who identified himself with the first some eighteen months after his death, engaged in activities of a more practical and propagandist kind until, after several years of partial success, he sank into oblivion.

From the Letter of an Alexandrian Merchant (1869)

I cannot, alas, satisfy your wish by sending you the last letter concerning our Lord which was written to me from Aden by Mori Yehudo Kuheil, because I have had all the written information relative to this holy matter carefully bound into a book. But I can give you a brief report based on those letters, as well as on accounts of more than twenty people, long known to me as trustworthy, from Sanaa, the native town of that man. During recent years they came to Alexandria either temporarily or permanently.

The man is extremely God-fearing, and is satisfied with very little; he never laughs but goes around with a bent head and is a great scholar. When he comes into a synagogue he seats himself very modestly in a corner and never in the seat of honor which is offered him. He never accepts an invitation to a meal, even on the occasion of a religious festival. Never has he in all his life accepted anything from the hand of man; rather he lives by the labor of his hands, for he is a leather worker making the artistically embellished tubes of the hookahs. Every day he works only until he has gained what is necessary for the support of his family, then he shuts up his shop and goes to study the Torah. At present he is about forty years of age.

One night our Lord, the prophet Elijah, appeared to him and bade him divorce his wife and go round all the villages of Yemen calling the people to repentance, and proclaiming that salvation was at hand and that utter repentance was necessary to save that generation from the birth pangs of the Messiah, the awful precursors of liberation. He was to go from hill to hill and valley to valley, as the prophet Elijah himself had done, that the prophet Isaiah's words might be fulfilled: "How beautiful upon the mountains are the feet of the messenger of good tidings, that announceth peace, the harbinger of good tidings, that announceth salvation; that saith unto Zion: thy God reigneth!"

He immediately parted from his wife, although there was love and concord between them and although their son was still attending the Torah school, and started on his wanderings; he went to the wildest and most desolate parts of Yemen. Wherever he went they wished to honor him with food and drink and clothing; but he never accepted anything, because so the prophet Elijah had bidden him. The bread which he ate he baked himself, the water he drank from a pumpkin shell he had with him; he never passed the night in a private house but always in a synagogue, and if anyone looked through the keyhole into the synagogue in which he slept, he saw a light as bright as day and it was as though many people were studying the Torah aloud.

When the scholars of Sanaa doubtfully asked him why it was that the message of salvation came just from the remotest corner of Jewry, he answered that the divine sparks that require rekindling are found in just this solitary place. Only when the shards of evil which enclose the divine spark have been shattered in this country will everything else go forward easily. (And this is the truth spoken in the "Prophecy of the Child": the Messiah will first reveal himself in the wilderness, and he will pass from the wilderness into the populated places.) Then they asked him where were the ten tribes which, according to the prophecy, should appear again in the time of redemption. To this he answered, that they are there, but people do not need them nor do they need the heroes of the "Sons of Moses." Everything must be accomplished through the power of repentance.

After the prophet Elijah had appeared to him, he became a new person in the knowledge of the Torah; the sources of all knowledge were opened to him; no hard problem remained unsolved for him; if one listened to him it was like a new Torah which nobody had heard and of which nobody had read in any book. He knew everything in the world, the names of all people, their being, and their character.

But the Muslims were jealous of Mori Yehudo and his message of redemption and they tried to murder him. But as often as a faction assailed him he felled them to the ground by the breath of his mouth; when he called the relatives to bury the dead they asked him on bended knees for pardon; whereupon in his mercy he brought the people back to life. If I were to describe what people undertook against him and how he guarded himself from his enemies, there would be no end to the tale. Because of him the Jews in Sanaa had to suffer dire persecution.

After three years he settled in the Jewish quarter of the town of Tinaam. There he shut himself up in a cell and gave orders that in no circumstances should he be disturbed. If people looked through the keyhole at night, again they saw the light as bright as day and caught the voices of many people studying the Torah. After ten or twelve days he walked out of his cell alone, just as he had entered it, and declared that he would climb such and such a mountain and there live in retirement for a year or more. Many years ago I myself had seen the mountain in my travels and learned that no human soul had ever climbed this dizzy height; for it is a place of demons and evil spirits. And just for this very reason Mori Yehudo chose the mountain as the place of his meditation, and he began to slaughter the wicked demons who dwelt there. The Imam of Sanaa, meanwhile, was disturbed by the increasing fame of Mori Yehudo, and when he heard that he lived all alone in the mountain fastness he put a high price on his head. Several officers with their men immediately set off to win this prize, and one day when the Mori appeared, they killed him by gunfire. Then they cut off his head and brought it to Sanaa, where the Imam let it hang on the gate of the Jewish town for three days. So the Muslims believed they had killed him. But the sister of the Mori and his son did not mourn for him because they knew for certain that he was still alive; for in fact he had prophesied all this exactly, and had explained in addition that he would only appear to suffer this in order that the Jewry of Sanaa might be freed from all persecution during his temporary disappearance from the world. And so it was.

After a year and a half had passed without his reappearance, I wrote to Aden asking his whereabouts. From there they informed me that it was now such a long time since his disappearance that many people had lost their belief in him and thought that they really had beheaded him. But shortly afterwards such and such a man came to me from Sanaa, who sold me a Torah scroll and bought some books from me, and stayed in my home for several days. This man told me in confidence that Mori Yehudo had shown himself again and that he was exchanging letters with the rabbis of Sanaa, but that, made wary by the former persecutions, they kept it very dark. I now made every effort to learn something more; but these efforts were soon rendered unnecessary, for two and a half years after his seeming death he quite openly appeared and took up his dwelling in a tower two hours' distance from Sanaa. From below one could see that he was holding a service with ten people, but who these people were is not known. Many non-Jews also believe in him and say that he is a prophet. But it is not necessary to describe all his doings, which are numberless. When he has accomplished God's will in Yemen, and come with God's help to Egypt, we shall see everything for ourselves. Peace be with you.

From the Great Missive of the False Messiah to the Doctors in Jerusalem

Thereafter I ascended Mount T. and there the Holy One, praised be He, worked great salvation through me; but the sin of Israel caused enemies to fall on me nonetheless, to kill me and to cut my head off, and all for the sake of Israel. But my Lord Elijah brought me back to life and from this day on ordered me to cease to occupy myself with the study of the Torah, and instead to wander unknown upon the earth. I went to all countries, and to Alexandria, too. There I fell ill for a month and there was none there who knew of me but a woman, by name, Berokho, who gave me food and drink. Afterwards my Lord Elijah cured me and we went traveling together, until we came to Mecca where we accomplished inexpressible things. Thereafter he ordered me to reveal myself to the people in the town of Tinaam, in Nissan of the year 5628 [1868], and I did as I was bidden. The Jews immediately denounced me and wished to kill me, but God saved me from all dangers. I stayed there about a year. Men came from everywhere to tempt and to test me. A villain and a great sorcerer from Israel, by name, Yehudo Shagi, wished to do me harm by his magic, but he achieved nothing, for God was with me whereas Shagi came in the name of Evil. Thereafter I left Tinaam in great honor and even a number of the non-Jews accompanied me. The ruler of Sanaa sent to pursue me, but his people could neither harm me nor any of my companions. Finally I settled in Tavila where I abode in great honor.

At that time the Lord Elijah ordered me to send messengers into all the cities of Israel to levy tithe; which I did. Some of the Jews paid the tax, but others mocked me. He who spoke and brought the world to life knows that I did not do it for myself, but for

Israel that they might have the means to free themselves from their slavery. When my reputation continued to grow and increase the ruler of Sanaa ordered the Jews there to hold a great service of prayer at the cemetery in order to destroy my power of action. But on the same day I went straight to Sanaa and appeared amongst them; the whole town was in a state of turmoil, and they wished to seize and kill me, but could not overcome me; everyone thought that they had seen me in another place, and so I fooled them all day. Since then they have greatly feared me. Then the rabbis of Sanaa sent a scholar named Yeshuo who was charged to dissolve my magical power; they thought indeed (God deliver us from evil) that I was a sorcerer. He hired Gentiles to get rid of me, but no sword could prevail over me, my neck was like a marble pillar.

This is some little part of what happened to me, Yehudo Kuheil. I thank God, who did not desert me and who fulfilled all that he had promised me. "When thou passest through the waters, I will be with thee, and through the rivers, they shall not overflow thee; when thou walkest through the fire, thou shalt not be burned, neither shall the flame kindle upon thee."

From a Letter from Aden (1869)

That night Mori Yehudo descended from the roof and sat next to the officer who had chopped off his head. The latter was most terribly frightened, and shouted aloud, "Shukri (so in Arabic they call Yehudo), what is all this about? Didn't I cut off your head with my own hand?"

"Don't excite yourself," replied the Mori, "I received a head on loan."

What an unexpected ending! Those who thought they had killed him were the first non-Jews to believe in him; leaving their homes they became his followers and went with him everywhere.

From the Testimony Given by a Rabbi from Sanaa Before the Rabbinate in Jerusalem in the Year 1870, After He Had Lost His Home and Possessions by Reason of His Having Denied the Messiah, and After Having Obtained a Hearing Neither in Yemen Nor in Egypt

In the year 5627 [1867] it was spread about that Mori Yehudo had risen from the dead and that he had made his dwelling in the city of Tinaam, a day's journey east of Sanaa. He had his former wife and his son come and live with him without being remarried, explaining that this separation had only taken place conditionally. When, however, a lot of gossip arose, he married her; also because the woman was pregnant by him. I have followed the affair closely, and found out from people who had known the man before that he bore no resemblance to the first Mori Yehudo who had been killed. When people asked him about that, he answered, "Just wait a little while, I'll get my old looks back eventually."

In any case, he has made no signs nor has he accom‑
plished any wonders, unless it be the following,
which has been several times reported: Every day
there come people sent to him from different places,
to whom he gives hospitality in his house; when there
are fifteen of them, for instance, he sends them only
enough food for four or five, and yet all are satisfied
and something is even left over. I heard this from
trustworthy people.

At Passover in the year 5628 [1868] the news was
spread that he would move with his host before Sanaa
on the eve of the new moon of Iyar. It was said that
he had an enormous following among the Muslims of
his district, as well as among the tribes of Reuben
and Gad, as many as sands on the seashore. Because
of this report, one ruler in that district wished to
have all the Jews in his territory massacred, and
asked the lords of the neighboring areas to sign a
document promising to do the same. The mayor of
Sanaa alone did not sign and defended our inno‑
cence before the others. After Passover the ruler of
Sanaa called together the rabbis and the heads of the
congregation and said to them: "You must pray to
God in this matter, for your prayers are wont to be
heard. If this man is sent from heaven, then we are
ready to do homage to him; but otherwise your
prayer will sap his strength, and he will cease from
stirring up the people." The congregation did as was
told them and stayed for three days at the cemetery,
praying at the graves of the pious; and on the third
day, the eve of the new moon of Iyar, all fasted, men,

women, and children. God heard their request and set an end to all the evil rumors. Of course, a great sum of money had to be paid to the mayor of Sanaa for his trouble. For a month nothing more was heard of Mori Yehudo. Then it was said that he had taken up residence in Tavila and there was collecting the tithe everywhere.

Not So Fast, Dear Mr. Messiah

This story is told in a Yemenite chronicle of the time of Sabbatai Zevi. However, it is familiar to all Yemenites in anecdote form, and it is told with a greater or lesser degree of embroidery.

Saada was a pious old widow who used to attend to the celebration of the Seder in the house of her neighbor. Now Saada knew that the Messiah comes on the night of the Passover; and since the four cups of unmixed wine whose use is prescribed for the Seder habitually threw her into a leaden sleep, she was terribly afraid that the Messiah would come and fly off with the whole congregation to Zion, while she remained alone in the Galut among the nations. Then she hit upon a wonderful idea. She made her bed in the doorway of her house, bound a cord round her right foot, and tied it round the neck of her donkey. The donkey would be sure to notice the Messiah's coming; he would smell the Messiah's donkey and bray aloud for joy. So, comforted, she fell asleep, full of the four cups but not of care. At midnight the donkey began to bray loudly—for this is just the time when donkeys do so—and dashed out through the door into the street, dragging his mistress behind him. She was filled with joy to hear the call of the Messiah and gladly allowed herself to be dragged along, only it was a little too rough and too strong; whereat she permitted herself to call out, "Dear Mr. Messiah, gently, gently!" The neighbors were awakened by this strange cry and were not a little surprised at the sight which greeted them. They stopped the donkey and shouted in the old lady's ear, "Saada, it's not the Messiah, it's only your donkey." But she paid no attention to the neighbors, only kept on calling out, "Not so fast, dear Mr. Messiah, not so fast!"

Bibliography

Erich Brauer's *Ethnologie der jemenitischen Juden* (Heidelberg, 1934) contains a bibliography of previous research. Later publications are my *Jemenica* (Leipzig, 1934); *Travels in Yemen* (Jerusalem, 1941); *Tales from the Land of Sheba* (New York, 1947); "Jewish Education in Yemen," in *Between Past and Future* (Jerusalem, 1953); "Communal Life of the Jews of Yemen," in *Mordecai Kaplan Jubilee Volume*, Hebrew Part (New York, 1953), pp. 43–61; and, especially, "The Language of al-Gades," *Le Muséon*, 73 (1960), 351–94, including stories and poems; see also Yehuda Ratzaby, "The Literature of the Jews of Yemen," in *Kirjat Sepher*, XXVIII (1953), 255–78, 396–409, with several later additions.

The mass exodus of 1949–50 gave rise to many publications. Joseph B. Schechtman, "The Repatriation of Yemenite Jewry," in *Jewish Social Studies*, XIV (1952), 209–24; Shlomo Barer, *The Magic Carpet* (London, 1953); Raphael Patai has paid special attention to the acculturation of the Yemenites in his *Israel Between East and West* (Philadelphia, 1953). On the same subject see my article "The Yemenite Jews in the Israel Amalgam," *Israel: Its Role in Civilization*, ed. Moshe Davis (New York, 1956). An extensive paper of mine on the religion of the Yemenites is included in *Religion in the Middle East*, ed. A. J. Arberry *et al.*, (Cambridge, 1969), ch. "Judaism," section 4. Joseph Zadoc, *BeSa'aroth Tēmān* (Tel-Aviv, 1956), is an illustrated, popular but detailed account of Operation Magic Carpet by an Israeli Yemenite who had taken a prominent part in it.

Scholars who have visited Yemen in recent times, including Carleton S. Coon, Carl Rathjens, E. Rossi, Hugh Scott, D. van der Meulen, and R. B. Serjeant, have paid attention to its Jews.

Four Yemenite immigrants to Israel have published books in Hebrew on Jewish life in Yemen, but mainly, or exclusively on that of the townspeople of the Higher Yemen, not that of the villagers of Lower Yemen, described in this paper: Joseph Kafih (Qāfeḥ), *Jewish Life in Sanaa, Halīkhōth Tēmān* (Jerusalem,

1961), 344 pp., ill., with map of Jewish Quarter of Sanaa; Amram Korah (Qōraḥ), *Saʿarat Tēmān* (Jerusalem, 1954), 188 pp., a few ill.; Yehuda Levi Nahum, *Mīṣefūnōth Yehūdē Tēmān* (Tel-Aviv, 1962), ill., esp. of old documents; Moshe Zadoc, *History and Customs of the Jews in the Yemen* (English sub-title of *Yehūdē Tēmān*) (Tel-Aviv, 1967), 272 pp., ill.